Iranian Cities

Published with the assistance of a grant
from the Iran-America Foundation

IRANIAN CITIES
Formation and Development

by
Masoud Kheirabadi

UNIVERSITY OF TEXAS PRESS, AUSTIN

Printed in the United States of America

First Edition, 1991

Requests for permission to reproduce material from this work should be sent to Permissions, University of Texas Press, Box 7819, Austin, Texas 78713-7819.

♾ The paper used in this publication meets the minimum requirements of American National Standard for Information Sciences—Permanence of Paper for Printed Library Materials, ANSI Z39.48-1984.

Library of Congress Cataloging-in-Publication Data

Kheirabadi, Masoud, 1951–
Iranian cities : formation and development / by Masoud Kheirabadi.
p. cm.
Includes bibliographical references and index.
ISBN 0-292-72468-3 (cloth : alk. paper)
1. Cities and towns—Iran. 2. Cities and towns, Islamic—Iran.
I. Title.
HT147.I6K48 1991
307.76'0955—dc20 90-47844
CIP

To the memory of my mother, who instilled in me the true value of education

CONTENTS

FIGURES

PREFACE

ALTHOUGH THERE ARE numerous studies dealing with Iranian culture and history, there are few texts focusing on Iranian cities. Of those few, many only describe the cities' histories and the lives of their founders, without any significant discussion of their forms. There is a noticeable gap in the literature (particularly in the English language) regarding the explanation of spatial patterns and the physical morphology of these cities. There is a need for more analytical studies that can explain the processes by which these cities have developed throughout Iranian history—studies that can provide readers with insights into the hows and whys of the morphology of traditional Iranian cities.

One objective of this book is to serve as a springboard for further study to fill this void. It is an attempt to study traditional Iranian urban forms primarily from a spatial point of view, analyzing the factors that have contributed historically to the site selection and morphological development of cities in Iran. I have tried to explain Iranian cities as the product of a multiple array of interrelated factors, including the physical environment of the Iranian Plateau, trade and historical events, and the religious and sociopolitical structures of Iran.

The primary objective of this book, however, is to enrich the understanding of Iranian cities and to enhance overall understanding of cities throughout the Middle East. Building on the works of others—both in Persian and in European languages—and utilizing my own field experience in Iran, I have searched for the rationale behind the physical morphology and spatial patterns of traditional Iranian cities.

Examining the traditional city's general form (compactness, uniform buildings, street form and orientation, courtyard houses) and its structural elements (bazar, residential areas), I discuss how the form of the city represents a response to Iranian Islamic culture and to the physical environment of the Iranian Plateau.

A book of this nature that attempts to cover such a broad subject over such a vast area can do justice neither to the history of urbanization in Iran nor to the geographic variations in city form throughout the country. However, it is my hope that this book, by presenting the subject in an analytical way, will serve as an instrument to broaden the horizon of research for similar studies of Iranian cities.

ACKNOWLEDGMENTS

I AM INDEBTED to many individuals who assisted me in the completion of this study. I particularly thank professors Ronald Wixman, Clyde Patton, Everett Smith, William Loy, and Richard Sundt of the University of Oregon for their guidance, support, and encouragement during this study. I am also indebted to several friends and colleagues who showed interest in editing drafts during the writing of this book. I thank Betty Grimshaw, Kimberly Keyes, Jane Erickson, David Marentette, Jonathan Smith, and Nola Long, who read over parts of my writing, and Marzieh Salari and Toraj Fasihi for assisting me with some of the illustrations. I also thank Dr. Mahmoud Saffari, for his constant encouragement, and Nancy DeSouza, who, with great care and patience, helped with the editing.

Many organizations were consulted during my 1984–1985 fieldwork in Iran for this study. I would like to express my thanks to the officials in the National Cartographic Center, the National Geographic Organization, and the Statistical Center of Iran for use of their materials. I am particularly grateful to the officials in the Architecture and City Planning Unit in the Ministry of Housing and Urban Development for graciously providing me with working space and access to their file of master plans for various cities.

I would like to thank several Iranian scholars, particularly, Professor Muhammad-Karim Pirnia of the University of Tehran Architecture and Urban Planning Department for his valuable advice and interest in my research.

I am also grateful to Professor Michael Bonine of the University of

Arizona, who carefully read the manuscript and made useful comments, and to Professor Kazem Tehrani of Portland State University for his help with transliteration. Although I have benefited from comments made by colleagues and friends, I alone am responsible for any flaws or inaccuracies in the book.

A NOTE ON TRANSLITERATION

FOR THE PURPOSE of consistency in spelling throughout the book, I have adopted the transliteration system used by the *International Journal of Middle East Studies.* However, the popular spelling has been used for words familiar in English (for example, Tehran instead of Tihran). With the exception of words widely used in English (such as Shiʿite), Persian (or other Middle Eastern) words are italicized. To make a Persian noun plural, an *s* is added to the singular form. In the case of Middle Eastern authors who have written in European languages, their own spelling of their names is used. For words shared by Persian (*fārsī*) and Arabic speakers, the Persian pronunciation is preferred regardless of the word's Arabic origin (*madrasih* instead of *madrasa* and *ḥusaynīyyih* instead of *ḥusaynīyya*). Diacritical marks are used for further clarification of Persian terms.

Iranian Cities

CHAPTER ONE

INTRODUCTION

THE PROCESS OF formation and development of cities worldwide has consistently been based upon the interrelation of the physical and cultural environments. The establishment of cities has resulted from various factors such as religion, economics, and military considerations. Historically, however, the cities that have survived over long periods are those built in areas with an available source of water and a relatively arable hinterland. The morphology and spatial patterns of these cities have gradually developed to satisfy the cultural needs of their populations and, at the same time, to respond to their surrounding environment. Thus, cities are the products of the interrelationship between their cultural and physical environments.

Iran is an excellent laboratory in which to study this interrelationship. The location and morphology of Iranian cities have long been influenced by both physical and cultural factors. The primary physical factors have been the hostile climate, the shortage of water, and the bowl-shaped physiography of the Iranian Plateau; the major cultural factors have been Iran's long religious and sociopolitical history and its rich cultural inheritance. Iran's location at a crossroads of major ancient trade routes and civilizations has also greatly affected the development of Iranian cities.

Among the numerous studies dealing with Iranian culture and history, there are very few that provide significant analysis of the cities of Iran. Many only describe their histories and the lives of their founders with little attempt to discuss their morphologies (e.g., Qumi 1934; Baihaqi 1938; Lockhart 1939, 1960; Arberry 1960; Balkhi 1971; Hunarfar 1978).

The spatial pattern and physical morphology of Iranian cities, however, have been studied by Heinz Gaube (1979). In his book *Iranian Cities,* he discusses the origins, historical development, and morphologies of the three Iranian cities of Herat, Isfahān, and Bam.

Although Gaube presents the spatial organization of these cities well, he does not give insights into the hows and whys of the patterns described.

There are also a few geographical studies dealing with specific Iranian cities (e.g., Bobek 1958; Planhol 1964a; Clarke 1966; English 1966a; Verlag 1966; Clarke and Clark 1969; Connell 1969; Bonine 1980), but with rare exceptions they do not deal specifically with the physical morphology of these cities. Michael Bonine is one of the few geographers who has taken this approach (a spatial point of view). In an article entitled "The Morphogenesis of Iranian Cities" (Bonine 1979), he searches for factors other than religion that have influenced their form and spatial patterns.

R. A. Frieden and B. D. Mann (1971, 1974), in their study of the city of Kirmān, search for factors that have influenced the orientation of streets and houses. They indicate that topography and water supply constitute the elementary principles of Iranian settlement geography; this idea is later emphasized and elaborated upon by Bonine (1979).

A few Iranian scholars (primarily architects and urban planners) have recently studied Iranian cities and written about them from an environmental point of view. Although these are valuable studies, they do not explain the impact of other cultural factors, such as religion and trade, on the development of these cities.

Mansour Falamaki's book *Siyrī dar Tajārub-i Marammat-i Shahrī: Az Viniz tā Shīrāz* (An Essay on Urban Conservation: From Venice to Shīrāz, 1978) contains a good discussion of traditional versus modern Iranian cities. Falamaki first studies the problem of urban conservation worldwide, giving examples from many older European cities. He then examines the same problem in relation to old Iranian cities and provides many examples.

Mahmood Tavassoli's work *Sākht-i Shahr va Miʿmārī dar Iqlīm-i Garm va Khushk-i Īrān* (Urban Structure and Architecture in the Hot Arid Zone of Iran, 1982) is another estimable study of Iranian cities, particularly the city of Yazd. Tavassoli studies the rationale behind the morphology of arid zone cities in Iran. Although the text of his book is scant, the accompanying maps and diagrams are useful in illustrating the themes.

Another comprehensive book published during the last decade concerning Iranian cities is *Shinākht-i Shahr va Maskan-i Būmī dar Īrān* (Understanding the City and Vernacular Dwelling in Iran, 1974), a joint effort by Mustafa Rabubi and Frangis Rahimiyyih. This is a study of Dizfūl and Shūshtar, two cities located in the hot and humid province of Khūzistān. Many maps and diagrams show the impact of the climate, sun, and wind on the design and development of housing and on other elements of the two cities.

Two more recent studies of Iranian cities, *Shahr-hā-yi Īrān* (Iranian Cities, 1987) and *Nazarī Ijamālī bih Shahr-nishīnī va Shahr-sāzī dar Īrān* (A General Study on Urbanization and Urban Planning in Iran, 1986), are valuable collections of articles by archaeologists, architects, and other researchers. These books, both edited by Muhammad Yusuf Kiani, are valuable mainly because of their illustration of Iranian cities through a number of air photos, maps, diagrams, and paintings. These are also among the few available sources that provide the reader with information about pre-Islamic Iranian cities.

Generally speaking, the common trend in the literature of Middle Eastern cities (including those in Iran) has been to view them under the title of "Islamic cities" (W. Marcais 1928; Sauvaget 1934, 1941; G. Marcais 1945; Pauty 1951; Von Grunebaum 1955; Planhol 1959; Roberts 1979; Blake and Lawless 1980). For many years, Middle Eastern cities were studied primarily from a religious point of view, and Islam as an "urban religion" was considered the definer of their form.[1] To explain the structural patterns of these cities, a model of the Islamic city—primarily based on case studies of Syrian and North African cities—was developed.[2] Figure 1 demonstrates elements of a traditional Islamic city and their spatial relations based on the model: the Friday Mosque forms the city's central core; religious schools (*madrasihs*), a public bathhouse (*ḥammām*), and the commercial district (bazar or bazaar) surrounding it. A hierarchical segregation of trade within the bazar, concentrated around the Friday Mosque, forms the basis of the spatial arrangement of the commercial district. Segregated residential quarters surround the core area of the city. The spatial organization and forms of the city were patterned, according to the developers of the model, primarily to respond to the requirements of Islam (e.g., Von Grunebaum 1955: 141–158; Planhol 1959: 9–10, 22–23).

The entire concept of the Islamic city has been questioned by A. H. Hourani in a more recent discussion of Middle Eastern cities.[3] Hourani argues that we cannot actually speak of something called the Islamic city over the wide area of the Muslim world. He questions whether we can explain any common features of cities in this vast region simply in terms of Islam and points out the necessity of searching for additional explanations.

This book goes beyond the Islamic city model—without underestimating Islamic influence on Iranian urban form—to look for various explanations to enhance our understanding of Iranian cities. My main objective is to study various factors that have been signifi-

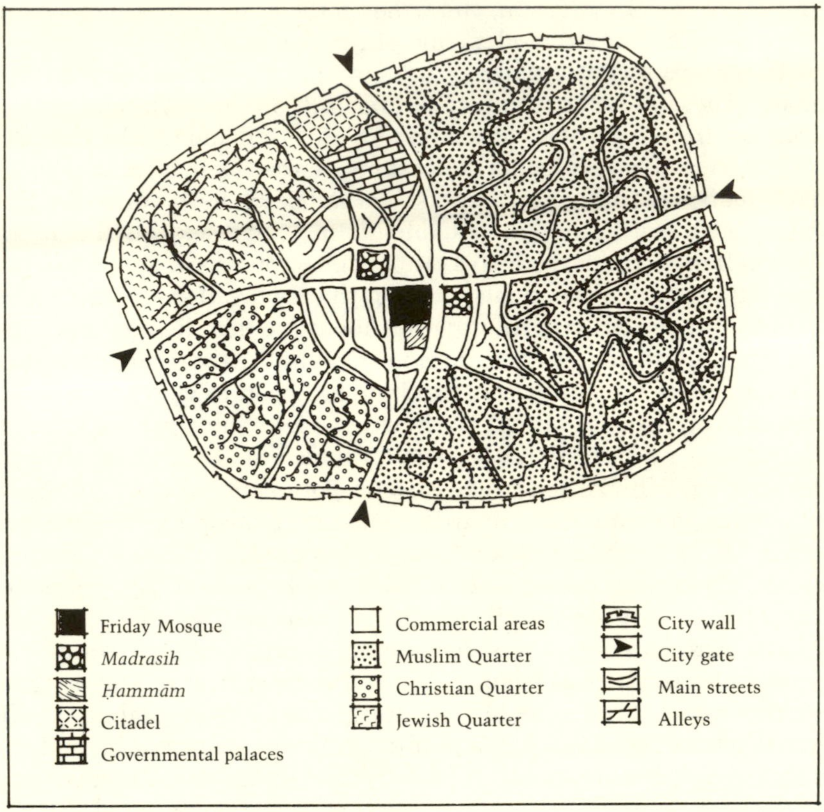

Figure 1. The Islamic city model.

cant in the formation and development of traditional Iranian cities and also, by a close examination of these cities, to seek the rationale behind their spatial patterns and physical morphologies.

Instead of emphasizing the impact of one factor (be it Islam, the environment, etc.) at the expense of all others, an alternative approach has been taken throughout this book: examining the impact of both environmental and cultural factors in the historical process of formation and development of Iranian cities.

The environmental (topography, climate, and availability of water) and cultural (religion, economy, and sociopolitical beliefs) factors studied in this book are so interrelated that mention of any one as the major definer of the physical shape of the city, without consideration of the others, is inadequate.

While the social configuration of the Iranian city is in conformity with the requirements of Islam, its physical morphology, to a great extent, is a rational cultural response to the natural environment, particularly to the topography and the climate of the Iranian Plateau.

For example, we cannot claim that a courtyard in an Iranian house is a structure built only to seclude women (a basic requirement in Islam). Although the courtyard serves this purpose adequately, Islam cannot be considered the only reason for the existence of the courtyard in Iranian cities.

One must concede that the courtyard existed in pre-Islamic Iran, as well as in non-Islamic regions. However, due to its functional conformity with Islamic requirements, the courtyard system remained the dominant pattern for houses in most Muslim cities even though its origin may be related to the necessity for defense and climatic considerations, rather than to Islam. Thus, defense and climate should be regarded as factors of equal importance to religion or other social beliefs in the separation of physical spaces by way of walls, courtyards, and so forth. What reinforces the importance of the courtyard as a morphological element in Middle Eastern cities, however, is its responsiveness to a hostile physical environment and its suitability to the region's cultural traditions.

Another example of this multiplicity of influences forming an Iranian city is the bazar. While the centrality of the bazar within the city emphasizes its economic and cultural importance, its form and appearance reflect the climatic characteristics of the Iranian Plateau. The bazar is covered to protect its users from the hot sun and thunderstorms common on the plateau; its lower level (relative to neighboring streets) increases air circulation by drawing the cooler, denser air into the bazar, keeping it cool during the hot summer afternoons.

Thus, the traditional Iranian city, like any other city of the Islamic world, is a response to the religious, economic, and cultural needs of its Muslim inhabitants. In addition, because of the severe arid conditions of the Iranian Plateau, it is also, to a great degree, a rational response to climatic characteristics.

With such considerations in mind, we may study the process of the formation and development of Iranian cities with reference to three major sets of factors: the physical environment of the Iranian Plateau, trade and historical events, and the religion and sociopolitical structures of Iran. These factors—being closely interrelated throughout the urban history of Iran—have greatly influenced the process of decision making in selection of the sites for Iranian cities and further development of their morphology and spatial patterns.

Information for preparation of this book was obtained primarily from on-site data collected during a fieldtrip to Iran (1984–1985), Iranian governmental and private agencies (air photos, maps, photographs, etc.), and the literature available through American libraries.

During the 1984–1985 academic year, field research was conducted in over thirty Iranian cities, some of which are presented as primary examples in this study. During each visit, a considerable amount of time was spent studying the old parts of the city and investigating the rationale behind their morphology. Professional geographers and urban planners in the Vizārat-i Maskan va Shahrsāzī (Ministry of Housing and Urban Development) were consulted and geographical and historical studies of master plans (*ṭarḥ-i jāmiᶜ*) for the development of various cities were examined.[4] Aerial photographs, city maps, and other illustrative data and documents produced by the two main cartographic organizations, Sāzimān-i Naqshih Bardārī-yi Kishvar (National Cartographic Center) and Sāzimān-i Jughrāfiyāyī-yi Kishvar (National Geographic Organization), were also used in the preparation of this work.[5]

Unless otherwise indicated, all photographs, maps, and other illustrations in this study are by the author. A great deal of library research was also conducted both in Iran and in the United States.

In summary, this study deals with traditional (preindustrial) Iranian cities. The term "traditional city" here refers to the city before the overall modernization of Iranian society that began after World War II. This, however, by no means indicates that this study lacks relevance for present Iranian cities. Traditional cities still form the old sections of many contemporary Iranian cities, and planners can benefit to a great extent from a close observation of their forms and the rationale behind them.

Although traditional Iranian cities can be found anywhere from western Mesopotamia to Soviet Central Asia, this study deals only with cities within the present boundaries of Iran, particularly cities in the plateau section of the country. Figure 2 shows the locations of cities mentioned throughout this study.

Organization was the most difficult aspect in the preparation of this study. The influences on urban development in Iran are so closely interwoven that the allotment of separate chapters to discussion of individual factors is difficult. Factors involved in the location, form, and function of various city structures should be discussed without continuously referring to other parts of the study. Taking these difficulties into account, the division of chapters according to influential elements remains the most practical and feasible way to pursue this study.

Figure 2. Iran.

Chapter 2 discusses the relationship between the natural environment of the Iranian Plateau and the formation and development of cities, examining the location of cities in relation to physical geography and seeking a rationale for the selection of city sites. The relationship between the internal structure of cities and the physical environment (particularly the climatic characteristics of the plateau) is also discussed.

Chapter 3 examines the formation and development of cities in relation to trade and history, considering the role of the economy and the impact of individual political leaders on the location and morphology of cities. The bazar, as the urban core of traditional Iranian cities, is studied in detail. Chapter 4 illustrates the impact of religion and sociopolitical structures on the form of cities, discussing the urban requirements of Islam (especially Shiʿite Islam) in relation to the spatial patterns and forms of cities. Urban elements resulting from societal and political structures of the city are also examined, along with the division of residential districts into segregated neighborhoods. Chapter 5 reviews the main themes of the study.

CHAPTER TWO

THE PHYSICAL ENVIRONMENT AND THE CITY

THIS CHAPTER EXAMINES the role of the physical environment of the Iranian Plateau, with its peculiar physiography and extended aridity, and the importance of qanats (subterranean aqueducts) in the historical formation and distribution of cities throughout the country. Later sections study the internal structure of the city and search for ways in which general appearance, streets, and housing patterns have traditionally reflected a rational cultural response to the natural environment (e.g., climatic characteristics, water, and topography) of the Iranian Plateau.

Five main questions are dealt with here.

1. What roles have the shortage of water and the bowl-shaped physiography of the Iranian Plateau played in the distribution of cities throughout the country?
2. How important have qanats been in the formation and development of cities?
3. In what ways have the physical forms of cities traditionally reflected a cultural response to the climatic characteristics of the Iranian Plateau?
4. What is the relationship between the street patterns and the cities' topography and water courses?
5. To what extent do the patterns of traditional houses respond to the climatic factors of temperature, wind, and precipitation?

City Sites and Physical Geography

Iranian cities primarily have been built in areas with an available source of water and a relatively arable hinterland. In most regions of

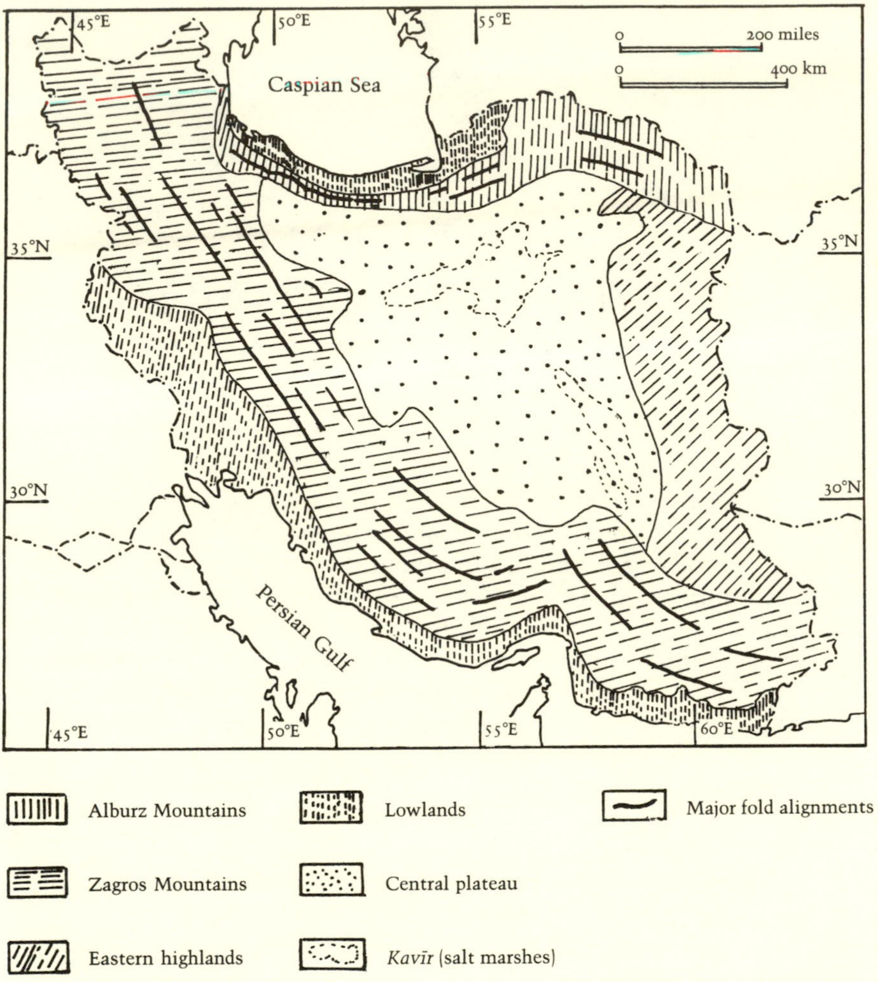

Figure 3. The physiography of Iran.

the plateau, cities obtain their water through qanats and are located at the foothills of mountain chains on alluvial fans or in intermountain basins. To a great extent, the distribution pattern of cities within the country has been influenced by the physical geography of the Iranian Plateau, particularly by the availability of water. To understand this, we need to review the major characteristics of Iran's physiography.

Iran extends between latitudes 25 and 40 degrees north and longitudes 44 and 63 degrees east, with an area of some 628,000 square miles (1,648,000 sq. km.). A mountainous country, with an average height over 3,000 feet above sea level, it is located between two major depressions: the Caspian Sea to the north and the Persian Gulf to the south. A complex of mountain chains rising steeply from these two depressions and mountain chains rising from the low-lying plain of Mesopotamia to the west enclose the interior basin.

Generally speaking, Iran can be likened to a bowl, with a high outer rim surrounding an irregular, lower interior. The inner central depression of Iran, which has been referred to as the Iranian Plateau (Fisher 1968; Ganji 1968), is surrounded by the Zagros and Alburz (Elburz) Mountains and the eastern highlands (fig. 3).[1]

The Iranian Plateau is a former seabed that dates from the Mesozoic era and found its present shape during the Quaternary period about 200,000 years ago. According to many geologists, it was formed and shaped by the uplifting and folding effects of three giant plates pressing against each other: the Arabian Plate, the Eurasian Plate, and the Indian Plate (Harrison 1968). The process of squeezing and pressing resulted in considerable folding at the edges, and some folding in the interior, which formed the present mountain ranges. The uplifting and folding of the plateau is a continuing process; the many recent earthquakes near or along the numerous faults (produced by subterranean shifts) attest to this process.

Physiography and Water

The peculiar bowl-shaped physiography has resulted in general dryness. Except for two strips in the northern and western sections, Iran consists mainly of dry lands and barren mountains. The Zagros Mountains, stretching from the northwest to the southeast, stand in the way of rain-bearing westerly winds. Similarly, the Alburz Mountains, extending from the northwest to the northeast and lying along the lower Caspian coast, obstruct the moist northerly winds, resulting in uneven distribution of precipitation over the plateau. Thus, while the bases of the mountains receive a considerable amount of moisture, the central basin of the plateau remains relatively untouched by any kind of precipitation. The amount of precipitation varies from over fifty inches on the Caspian coast to less than two inches in the desert areas (Ganji 1968). In the most arid regions of Iran, the annual rainfall is below four inches and the relative humidity rarely exceeds twenty percent. Figure 4 shows the distribution of precipitation for Iran.

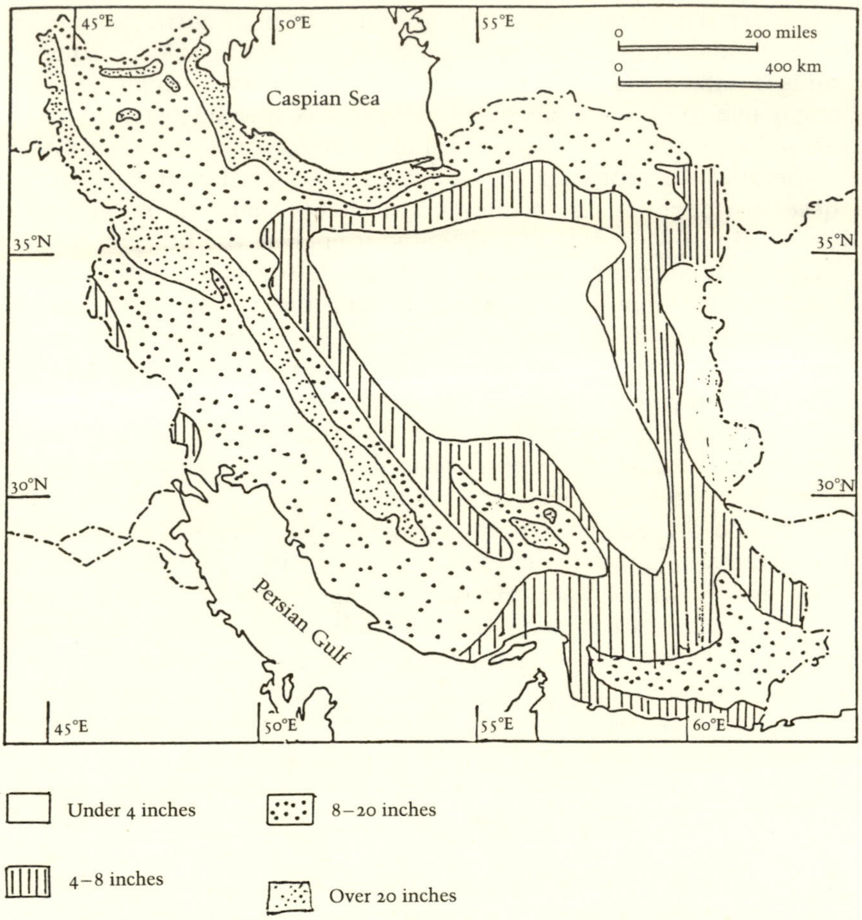

Figure 4. Approximate average annual precipitation in Iran (adapted from Smith 1971).

Distribution of rainfall throughout the country is directly influenced by the presence of mountains. However, from the northwest to the southeast, this relationship becomes less apparent. These orographic effects have resulted in a vivid contrast between relatively moist spots and rain shadows that can be seen in most parts of the country. This contrast is also pronounced in the density of hu-

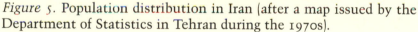

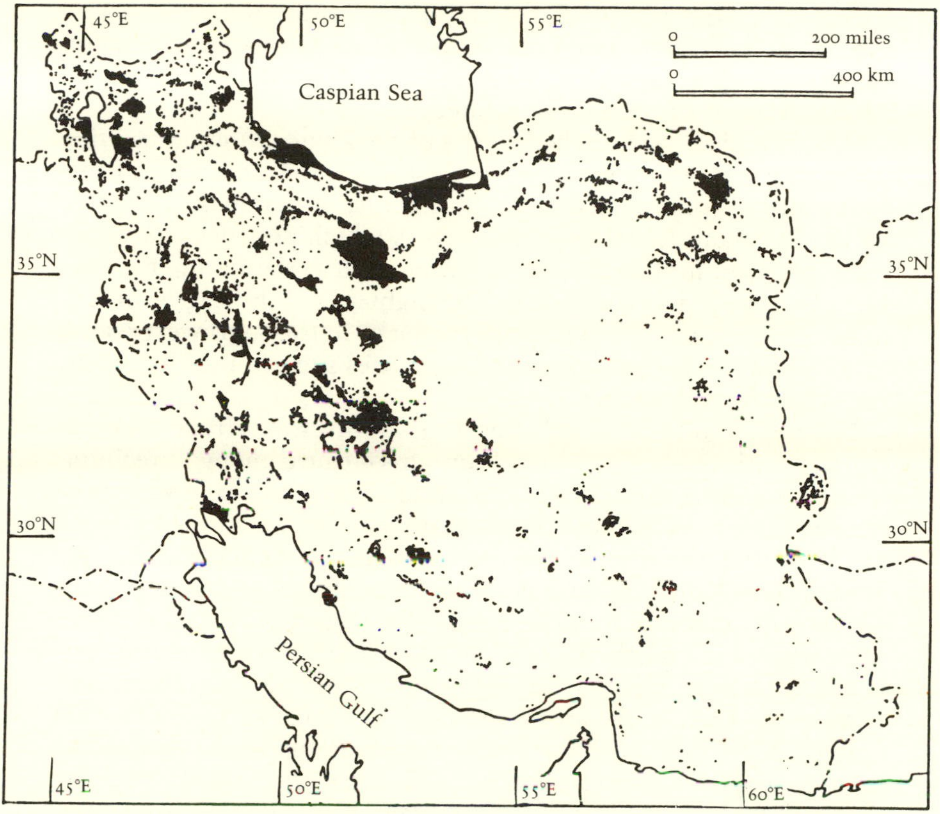

Figure 5. Population distribution in Iran (after a map issued by the Department of Statistics in Tehran during the 1970s).

man settlements; most of them occur on the sides of the mountains where access to water is possible. Iran's population distribution pattern is seen in figure 5.

Water and Settlements

Due to the general dryness of the country, water has always been an influential factor in distributional patterns of settlements and in the intensity of human activity throughout Iran. A comparison of the two maps in figures 4 and 5 aptly illustrates this relationship. The eastwardly traveling cyclonic depressions carry enough moisture to support sizable populations in western regions of Iran, mainly along the western slopes of the Zagros Mountains. They also provide a dependable supply of surface water for some intermountain basins where large cities such as Tabrīz, Hamadān, Kirmānshāh, Khurram-ābād, and Shīrāz are located.

Rivers originating from high zones of the Zagros Mountains bring prosperity and beauty to the cities they irrigate. An example of this is the city of Iṣfahān. Iṣfahān, with its large hinterland, is irrigated by the Zāyandih-Rūd (Life-giving River), which provides a fascinating focal point for the city. Other rivers, such as the Kārūn, the Karkhih, and the Diz, originate from the highlands of the Zagros Mountains, irrigate the fertile plain of Khūzistān in the southwest region of the country, and pass through large cities such as Dizfūl, Shūshtar, Ahvāz, and Ābādān.

The moist northerly winds traveling southward—after coming in contact with the high Alburz Mountains—cause enough precipitation to support a considerable population in the coastal lowlands of Māzandarān and Gīlān provinces, mainly along the northern slopes of the Alburz Mountains. The coastal plains of the Caspian Sea receive a considerable amount of rainfall year round; this makes them climatically different from the rest of the country. They also receive the runoff of the northern slopes of the Alburz Mountains and contain large rivers such as the Safīd-Rūd, Harāz, Bābul, Tijan, and Gurgān. As a result, the area is presently the most suitable place for crop production—particularly rice, a main staple in the diet of the Iranian people. The area includes such large cities as Rasht (near the Safīd-Rūd), Sārī (along the Tijan River), Bābul (on the bank of the Bābul River), and Gurgān (on the Gurgān River).

As seen in figure 4, regions with a mean annual rate of precipitation less than eight inches constitute the major portion of the country. Considering the fact that this amount of water is inadequate for dry agriculture, one might question the existence of many Iranian cities south of the Alburz and east of the Zagros Mountains. The answer lies in the availability of subsurface water reservoirs that have traditionally been used by the Iranian population.

The presence of subsurface water reservoirs is related to the geological history of the Iranian Plateau. Heavy rains and violent floods of the glacial period resulted in severe erosion of mountain rocks, which were pulverized and transported to the foothills and nearby plains. Because these lands contain irregular layers of sand and pebbles, they form considerable water reservoirs. The particular surface configuration of the Iranian Plateau and the available irrigational technology through qanats allow this water to be moved to the lower lands to be used for drinking or irrigation. Qanats are subterranean aqueducts that collect groundwater at the foot of mountains and carry it, by gravity, through gently sloping tunnels into alluvial materials, to the fields and settlements (figs. 6 and 7; for a detailed discussion of qanats and their construction, see also appendix A).[2] Alluvial fans are major products of the surface configuration of the Iranian Plateau.

The internal depression of the plateau is composed of a series of smaller basins that are surrounded by the highlands. The steep upland zone in Iran varies from hundreds to thousands of meters and is the area of maximum erosion activity. This erosion includes the processes of weathering, mass movements on the steep slopes, and considerable fluvial activity along the major valley systems. The process of weathering occurs mainly through freeze-thaw action resulting from the extreme temperature fluctuations.

Located at the lower margins of the upland zone is the alluvial fan zone, which, in its continuation into the less steep plain, forms the best agricultural land of Iran. This is a zone formed by the depositional action of running water bringing the eroded materials from the uplands by fluvial and mud-flow activity. Some of the fine deposits—primary silt and clay—are carried away from the zone by wind and water and are redeposited on the *kavīr* (barren desert), which is distinguishable by its flatness (a slope of less than one degree) and its whitish salt crust in hot seasons. The Dasht-i Lūt and Dasht-i Kavīr (*dasht* means an open land in Persian) in Iran are the best examples of these *kavīr*s.

Most Iranian settlements are located within the large alluvial fans in the piedmont zone between the mountains and deserts. These include cities such as Tehran, Qazvīn, and Kirmān. Some of these settlements are located on large alluvial valleys on the desert fringe. Shīrāz is a good example of this type. As stated previously, the majority of these settlements receive an annual precipitation that is less than the minimum required for crop production, and most of them are not supplied by any major rivers with sufficient discharge for agricultural uses. However, the subterranean aqueducts or qanats supply the source of water for these settlements.

The water falling on the uplands runs off the bedrock; some of it seeps into the gravel and sands of the alluvial fan and finds its way toward the center of the basin. Water near the periphery of the basin, at the foot of the mountain, is fresh and sweet (i.e., not saline), with the water table deep beneath the surface. At the center of the basin, water becomes more stagnant and mineralized, with the water table very close to the surface. Here the settlements are provided with fresh water from the periphery through qanats, which collect ground-

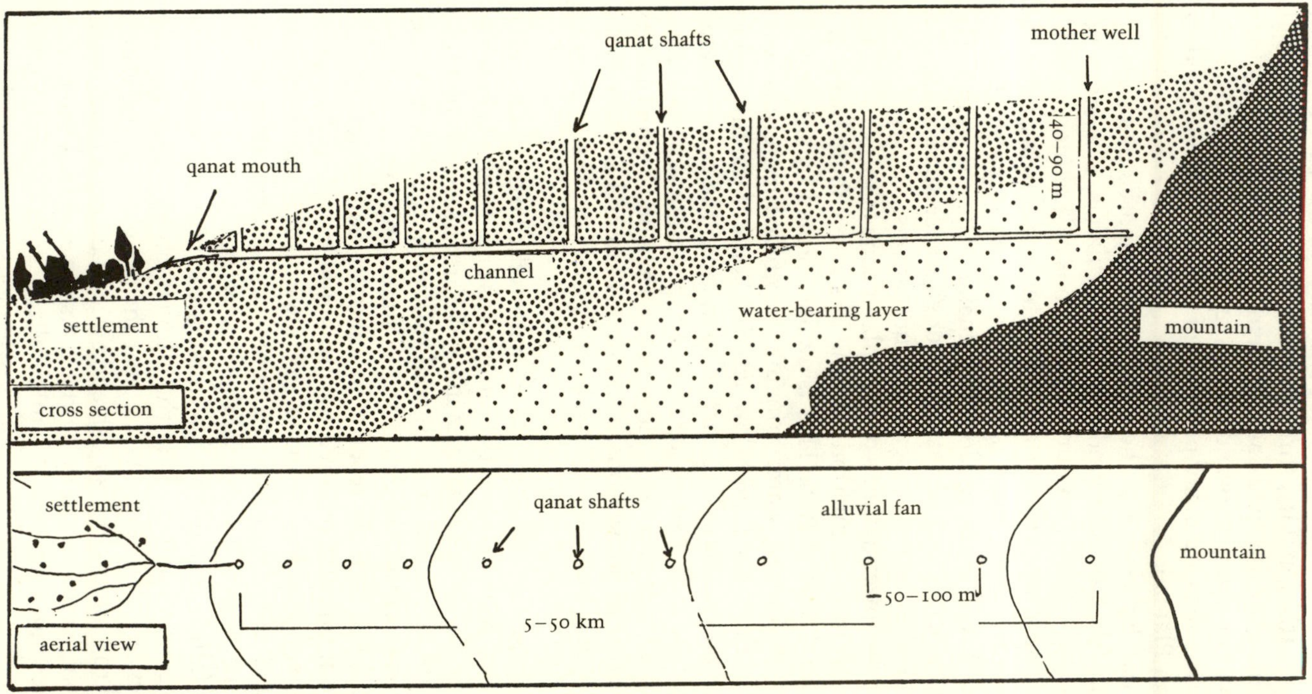

Figure 6. Diagram of a typical qanat.

Figure 7. Qanats in Kirmān; qanats are seen as continuous lines of mounds (1956 aerial photograph, National Cartographic Center, Iran; original scale 1 : 6,000).

water at the foot of the mountain and carry it by gravity through gently sloping tunnels to the fields or settlements (see fig. 6).

Due to the importance of qanats as the only source of water, the distribution of settlements on alluvial fans in the desert margins of Iran is closely related to the distribution pattern of qanat systems. For example, English (1966a), in his study of the Kirmān (Kerman) Basin, endorses this point by illustrating the large settlements located high on the alluvial fans, beyond the catchment basin drained by Kirmān city's qanats. Major cities are located where the major qanat systems are. Figures 8 and 9 demonstrate the relationship between qanats and settlements in the Sāvih Basin. Sāvih is located near the base of the Shāhpasand Mountains and, like neighboring settlements, receives its supply of water through qanats, deriving water from underground reservoirs at the bases of these mountains. In most instances in the Iranian Plateau, settlements follow the qanat belt that roughly encircles the great *kavīr* of the central basin (Beaumont 1971).

It must be mentioned that qanats cannot be built in all arid regions of the plateau, because their construction is closely related to the physical setting of the terrain. They require a groundwater source located either at the foot of an adequately watered mountain or in a place reachable by streams and rivers coming from highlands with sufficient precipitation. This is the main reason for the lack of qanats, and therefore settlements, in the central *kavīr*s of Iran.

The hot summer days, cold winters, and black, muddy marshes also present dangers in the central *kavīr*s of Iran. For a long time, no travelers would even dare to cross them. The settlement of central Iran is, to this day, restricted to isolated oases and the flanks of small mountain chains where water is available.

Another factor preventing the formation of cities in the central desert is wind. Some winds carry with them sand and dust; they damage crops and livestock, cover roads and houses, and continually change the surface features of the land. For example the *bād-i ṣad-uw-bīst rūzih* (wind of 120 days), which originates over the central *kavīr*s during summer days, is hot and violent, carrying abrasive sand particles. It blows toward the provinces of Sīstān and Balūchistān, destroying plants and vegetation, stripping away the soil, and damaging the buildings and livestock (Scharlau 1961; Fisher 1968).

Although the physical geography of the Iranian Plateau has a significant impact on the location of cities, it alone does not account for the presence and location of settlements. One cannot ignore cultural factors, such as major trade routes, military and strategical re-

Figure 8. The city of Sāvih; a view from point A on the map in fig. 9, showing the townsite of Sāvih in relation to the Shāhpasand Mountains to the northwest.

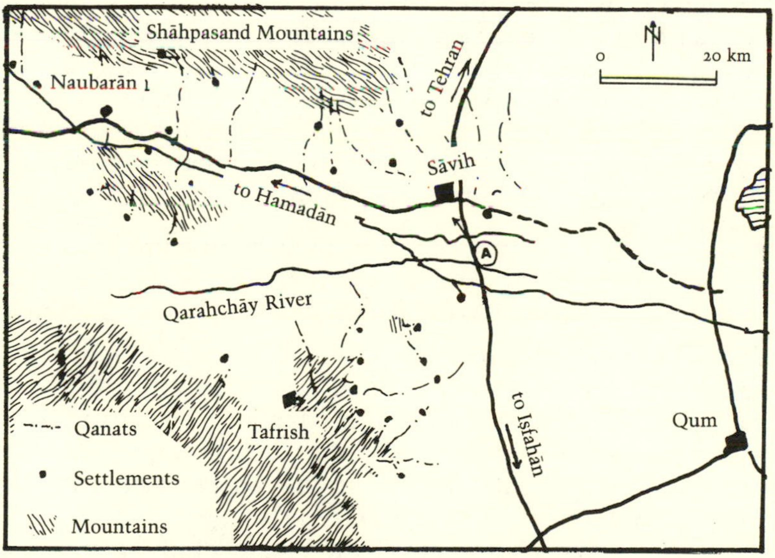

Figure 9. Qanats and settlements in the Sāvih region (1974 map of Iran by the National Geographic Organization, Iran; original scale 1 : 1,000,000).

quirements, and religious and political considerations. The impact of these cultural elements is discussed in the following chapters.

Thus far, the roles of the bowl-shaped physiography of the Iranian Plateau, water shortages, and qanats in the distribution of cities throughout Iran have been examined. The remainder of this chapter investigates the impact of the physical environment on the internal structures of Iranian cities.

City Structures and the Physical Environment

The physical morphology of the traditional Iranian city is, to a great extent, a cultural-historical response to the natural environment, especially to the climatic conditions of the Iranian Plateau. As stated previously, with the exception of two narrow regions (one along the Caspian Sea and the other along the western slopes of the Zagros Mountains), Iran is an arid country. Its extreme climatic conditions are characterized by a shortage of water, higher evaporation than precipitation (resulting in low humidity), intense solar radiation (especially during hot summer days), high diurnal and seasonal temperature ranges, torrential—but sporadic—spurts of precipitation, and damaging dust and sandstorms.

Through the millennia, the urban form of Iranian cities developed to cope with such climatic conditions. To adjust to the hostile climate, traditional Iranian urban planners learned to minimize the direct impact of solar radiation, to soften the blow of harmful and unpleasant winds, and to optimize the use of shade, breeze, and water. The planners' objectives were achieved by adopting a compact urban form, developing special street and alley patterns, and designing houses with courtyards.[3]

Compact Urban Form

In contrast to modern Iranian cities, which are simply copies of the contemporary, diffused European and American cities, the traditional Iranian city is concentrated and homogeneous in its buildings, combining diverse land uses in a tight relationship with each other. Figure 10 illustrates the traditional compact city of Shīrāz surrounded by a sprawling, modern city.

While the primary reasons for the development of the early compact Iranian cities may have been necessities such as defense, social cohesiveness, land conservation for agricultural use, and optimal size, the compact system as the dominant urban form in arid regions

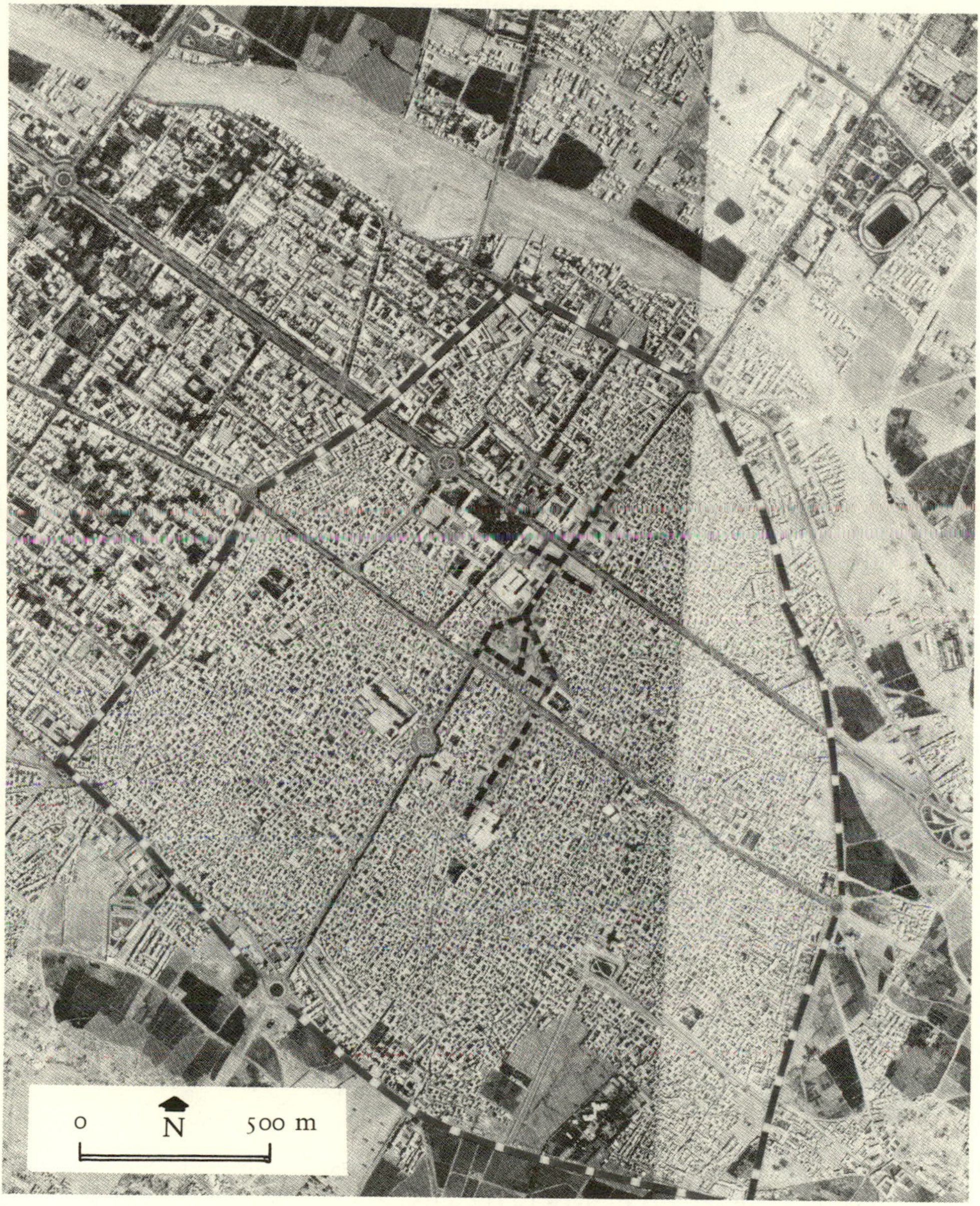

Figure 10. The traditional city of Shīrāz is easily distinguished from the sprawling new urban areas (1967 aerial photograph, National Cartographic Center, Iran; original scale 1 : 20,000).

of Iran probably has been maintained as a result of its climatic advantages.

The compact traditional city has the potential to reduce the climatic stress considerably and to ameliorate microclimatic conditions. It minimizes the amount of building surface exposed to direct solar radiation, thus reducing the total heat gained and providing more comfort for its inhabitants. In single-family dwellings totally detached from surrounding structures (popular in present suburban residential zones of modern Iranian cities), a large amount of wall and roof area is exposed to the direct sun. In comparison, a traditional Iranian house, attached to its neighbors by three or four walls, minimizes exposure. In the compact city with a high density of residential areas, most external pedestrian spaces are sheltered from direct sunlight (Olgyay 1963; Golany 1982, 1983).

Compactness also results in the proximity of land uses within the traditional city. Land uses are physically integrated and at the same time functionally separated. The land pattern is integrated in such a way that the economic, educational, religious, and other public centers intermingle with residential land. At the same time, the principal access network connecting residential areas to the bazar complex acts as the buffer zone between residential (private) and nonresidential (public) areas.

The climatic advantages of a compact urban form can be summarized as follows.
A compact system:

1. reduces direct radiation and evaporation;
2. minimizes heat gain during the day and heat loss at night;
3. provides shade and cool air;
4. makes human movement easier within the city;
5. breaks both strong hot day winds and cold night winds; and
6. reduces the harmful effects of dusty storms.

In addition to responding to climatic stress, a compact system offers many other advantages to the city: a noticeable reduction of the infrastructure network and the transportation system; minimizing energy consumption by employing the forces of nature such as passive cooling systems; easy accessibility; retaining land for other uses such as agriculture; social cohesiveness; and, finally, conserving the environment by employing passive cooling systems (Golany 1983).

To cope with these environmental problems, traditional Iranian cities minimized empty space, had buildings of uniform height, and contained narrow, sometimes winding streets. Covering bazars and alleyways was another means of responding to these harsh climatic conditions. Early Iranian planners also recognized the importance of orientation to the wind and sun and of water elements.

Traditional Iranian cities, particularly cities of central Iran, contain relatively few large open spaces. This is due to the fact that in a hot and arid city (like most Iranian cities) any large empty space, because of its direct exposure to the sun, generates heated air during the day and cold air at night. An open space, therefore, accelerates the climatic stress, unless it is shaded by trees or contains a body of water.

In addition, as can be seen in aerial pictures of traditional Iranian cities, the height of the buildings (with the exceptions of some mosques or minarets) is uniform throughout the city (see fig. 11). This permits the free movement of air above the city. When a few tall buildings stand higher than a number of shorter ones, air is diverted downward, resulting in the development of unwanted turbulence. In hot and arid Iranian cities, which receive frequent strong winds, the presence of high-rise buildings creates serious problems of turbulence.

Streets and alleys within a city also function as channels for air movement and heat exchange; therefore, they maintain a significant role in establishing the city's climate. In the hot arid cities of Iran, wide, straight streets function as channels for hot dusty winds during the day and for cold winds at night. Sandstorms blowing over the city flow unimpeded through wide, open streets, creating problems for pedestrians. The disadvantage of wide, straight streets is more visible during hot summer days when the air near the surface is heated and rises in funnel-shaped dust currents that blow around the city within the large open spaces. A climatically well-adjusted traditional street is seen in figure 12; figure 13 clearly demonstrates the tremendous vulnerability of the wide boulevards to these dust currents. This problem is evident in the modern parts of many Iranian cities, as well as throughout the rest of the Middle East.

Narrow streets and alleys, surrounded by tall walls oriented toward pleasant winds, are well shaded during the hot summer afternoons. The advantages of the traditional pattern are that the streets:

1. retain humidity and reduce daily temperature;
2. protect inhabitants against the harmful winds and are open to pleasant winds; and
3. are shaded and cool during the day and warm at night.

A

B

Figure 11. Uniformity of buildings in Sabzivār: A, standing at the top of Imāmzādih Shuʿayb's minaret to the south of the city, looking north; B, standing at the top of Imāmzādih Yaḥyā's minaret at the center of the city, looking west.

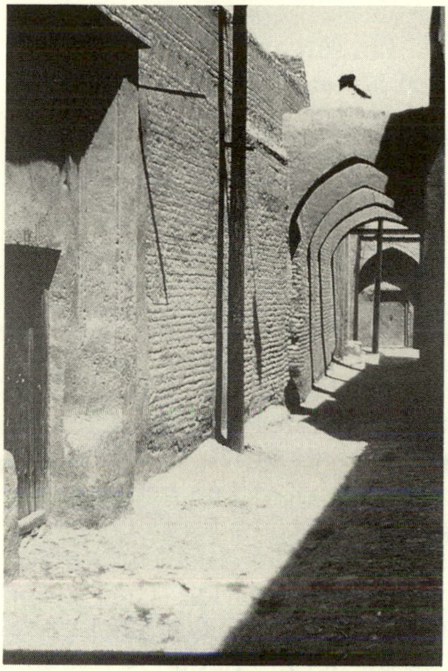

Figure 12. Typical street in a traditional Iranian city.

Figure 13. Wide boulevard in Iṣfahan (personal collection of Sally Butler).

Covered bazars and enclosed passageways protect the inhabitants of traditional Iranian cities against the hot sun, turbulent winds, and torrential downpours. The linear bazar is usually covered by a series of mud domes and its floor level is lower than the neighboring areas. This creates a flow of cool air into the bazar (cool air is denser than warm air, so it descends), resulting in a more comfortable environment. The covered bazar with its circulating air creates a pleasing microclimate that attracts city dwellers, particularly during hot summer afternoons.

Roofs are mainly made of mud or sun-dried bricks. For the hot, arid regions of Iran, mud domes function more effectively than flat roofs in terms of reducing solar heat. The form of the dome (spherical or cylindrical) increases the total surface area of the roof, resulting in the spread of intensity of solar radiation over a larger area, thereby decreasing the average heat of the roof and its transmission to the interior. A domed roof, in addition to being partially shaded from the sun for most of the day, allows winds to cool its surface easily and thereby minimizes the intensity of radiation. The form of the dome also causes an increase in the height of the ceiling for the room below, providing more space for the hot interior air to rise and exit through the roof.

When the double dome is used (i.e., one dome inside another), the space between the inner and outer dome acts as an insulation layer. On summer days, when the outer dome becomes very hot, the inner dome stays cool. The circulation of air between the two domes, through openings between them, reduces the radiation problem and cools off the area beneath the roof (Tavassoli 1983).

Planners of traditional Iranian cities were aware of the significance of the sun and the wind in architecture and city planning. Their objective was to establish the optimum orientation with regard to the sun at various hours of the day during different seasons and the direction of prevailing winds. Utilizing the wind was particularly practical in cities in which the dusty unpleasant winds come from different directions than the cooler breezes. Several cities of Khurāsān and central Iran provinces illustrate this situation. City structures (such as passageways) when possible were usually oriented to the favorable winds and shielded from the unfavorable ones (Bavar 1983).

Water through qanats made the life and formation of cities possible throughout most of the Iranian Plateau. At the city scale, as shown below, water often defined the order of main access networks. In traditional Iranian cities, water was also used as a cooling element, often appearing in the form of *jūb*s (or *jūy*s, open ditches) running along the streets and center lines of alleys. These also added to the visual appeal of the city. Wherever possible, streets were lined with trees, receiving their water through these *jūb*s (still seen in many Iranian villages and some smaller cities). Water was also used, in the form of pools at the center of courtyards, for evaporative cooling as well as for recreational purposes.

Street Patterns

The strong desire for privacy and tranquillity in residential units led traditional Iranian cities to evolve into two major sections: public and private. The bazar complex, and all its related spaces, formed the center of public life, where all public and social activities took place (the bazar is discussed in detail in the following chapter). The residential zone was the private section of the city, where a peaceful atmosphere prevailed (Ardalan and Bakhtiar 1979).

Spatially, the entire city was tightly packed; the bazar and residential areas were so physically integrated that the study of one, as an independent physical entity separate from the other, is nearly impossible.

Residential areas were connected to the bazar by small, narrow alleys (known as *kūchih*s in Persian).[4] These *kūchih*s wound through residential areas, providing an intricate, intersecting pattern of access between residences and businesses. They were bordered on both sides by the high walls of residential compounds, uniform in color and texture and usually made of mud mixed with straw. The walls were windowless, with only an occasional door providing an entrance to the compound. Some *kūchih*s could be quite lengthy, starting at the bazar and continuing through residential neighborhoods (occasionally joined or crossed by other *kūchih*s) until they reached a city gate or ended at the city wall. More typically, the *kūchih* ended at a neighborhood center—an open space containing a few shops and public buildings. Neighborhood centers are studied in chapter 4, where the impact of social structure on the form of the city is discussed.

Some *kūchih*s coming off the bazar were wider than others; these were often called *guzar*s, which literally means pathways. A *guzar* that ran in a straight line was called a *rāstih*, meaning a straight lane. *Guzar*s and *rāstih*s had the shape and function of streets rather than alleys and were more common in larger Iranian cities such as Tehran, Iṣfahān, and Shīrāz. Such streets were joined along their routes by the smaller *kūchih*s. Usually some public buildings (such as mosques or other religious buildings, public bathhouses, tea-houses, etc.) were located along these streets. A *guzar* was often named after an influential person who once lived there. Many examples of this can still be seen in Tehran around the bazar complex, such as Guzar-i Lūṭi Ṣāliḥ, named after Lūṭi Ṣāliḥ, a local hero known for his generosity.

Branching off the *kūchih*s were many small blind alleys (known as *bunbast*s in Persian). Like *kūchih*s, *bunbast*s were bounded on both sides by high, windowless walls, broken only by an occasional door into a residential compound.

The Traffic Network Hierarchy

The residential byways ultimately tended to funnel into the bazar, which then served as the main thoroughfare for the city. The bazar also provided access to areas outside the city; its termini were the city gates. To find a house in the traditional Iranian city, a visitor would walk through the bazar to the appropriate *guzar* or *rāstih*, and then to the appropriate *kūchih*s and, if necessary, to the *bunbast* on which the destination house was located. Very rarely were there alternative routes through the city. Thus, a distinct hierarchy of street size and function formed the traffic network of the traditional Iranian city (Frieden and Mann 1971).

Based on this description of street networks, a model of the access system for traditional Iranian cities can be devised utilizing all elements of the traffic network. This model may not totally fit all traditional Iranian city traffic networks, particularly those of smaller towns. However, it can, with some minor variations, explain the spatial hierarchy dominating the traffic network in traditional Iranian cities.[5] This model traffic network in its totality includes five major elements: the bazar, *guzar*s, *kūchih*s, *bunbast*s, and *hashtī*s (see fig. 14).

The main linear bazars are the primary thoroughfares that pass through the city and connect the city's gates. These are the most important and crowded streets of the city. They rarely contain any residential units, but do provide access to other streets and *kūchih*s that run through residential areas.

*Guzar*s and *rāstih*s are the primary streets of the city; they come off the *rāstih-bāzār*s (linear stretches of bazars), run through the residential zones, and usually end at neighborhood centers. Along these streets, especially where they intersect at a neighborhood center, minor public buildings are located. (Now most *guzar*s have been widened and replaced or crossed by new streets to fit motor vehicles.)

*Kūchih*s, or secondary access routes, are the narrow alleys that

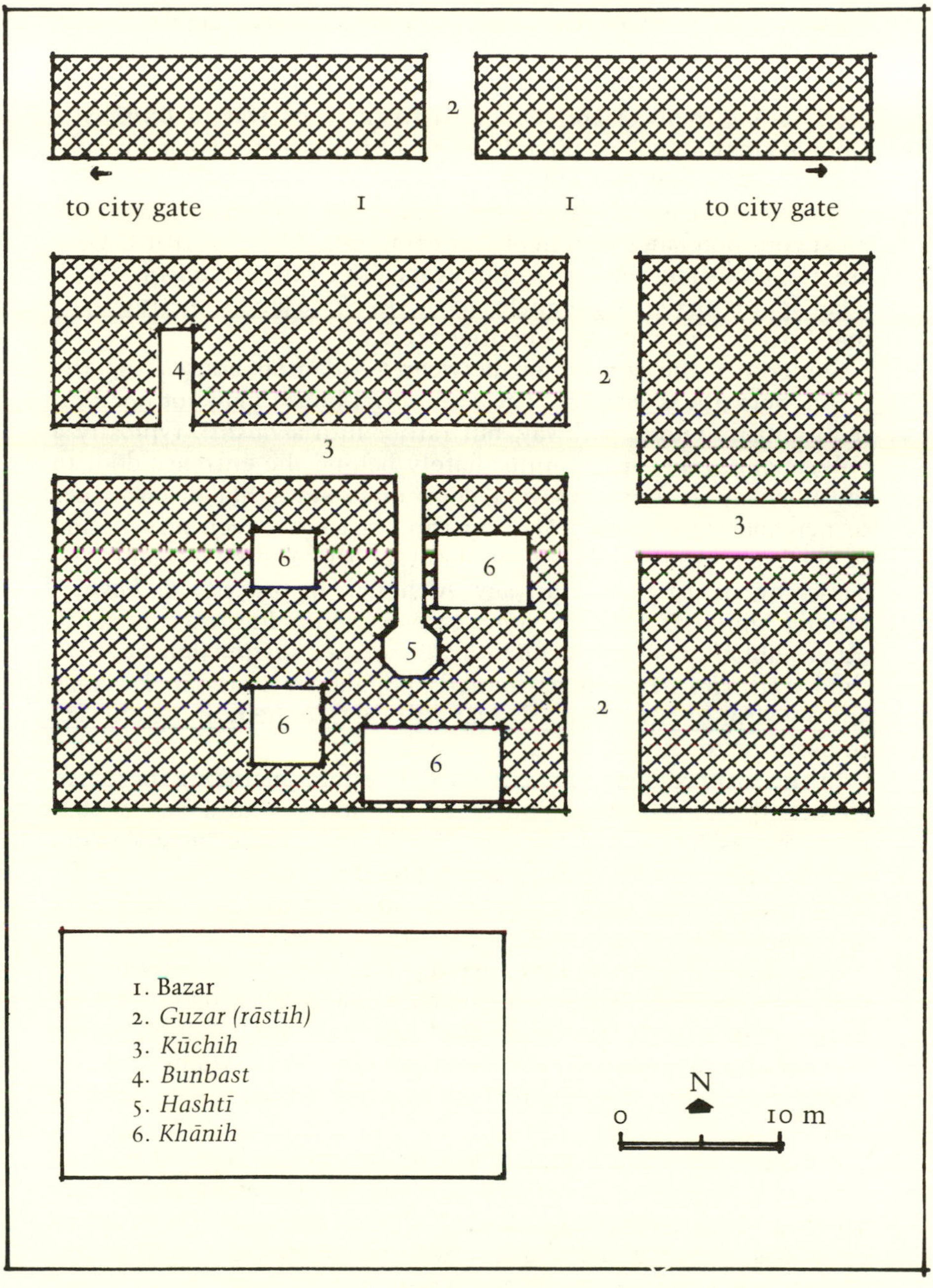

Figure 14. Model of the access system in the traditional Iranian city.

branch off the primary streets and wind through the neighborhoods, normally ending at another primary street. They have an average width between two and four meters; houses either are located directly along them or are connected to them by way of *bunbast*s. *Kūchih*s may branch off directly from the bazar instead of being connected through primary streets.

*Bunbast*s, or tertiary access routes, are blind alleys that form the most common lanes seen in plans of traditional Iranian cities. They are numerous and seem to run in every direction. *Bunbast*s branch off at approximately right angles to the *kūchih*s (and sometimes primary streets), providing residential access.

Sometimes the connection between residential houses and the traffic network is indirect. The residential house may not open directly into a public pathway, but rather into a *hashtī*, typically a polygonal covered space, immediately behind the entrance door to the alleyway.[6] It contains several doors on its sides that are entrances to neighboring houses. This transition space between private and public life prevents a direct visual contact between the residents and passersby, offering more privacy. Although in this model *hashtī*s lead off *bunbast*s, there are other cases in which *hashtī*s connect to other public ways such as *kūchih*s, *guzar*s, or *rāstih*s (but never to the bazar). *Hashtī*s were particularly popular in Khurāsān Province and a visitor to cities like Sabzivār still can see them in the old sections of the town.

In an idealized hierarchic circulation system (including these five elements), the access system, therefore, starts with a *hashtī* that connects residences to a *bunbast*. The *bunbast* feeds into a *kūchih*, which in turn merges with a primary street (*guzar* or *rāstih*). Finally, the primary street leads to the main street of the city (the bazar), providing access to the outer city and interurban routes.

Therefore, the circulation system, consisting of different-sized pathways and the main street (the bazar), was not random, but rational in its design. This view does not, however, conform to the popular ideas expressed in the West that describe the traffic network of Islamic cities of the Middle East as a maze of irregular, twisting lanes.[7]

Studying the configuration of the old streets and lanes in existing plans of Iranian cities reveals the fact that the streets in most cities follow a rough geometric pattern. Although this may not be apparent at first glance, a careful inspection and comparison of the streets reveals order underlying the street network of these cities (Bonine 1979).

The basic geometric configuration is formed by a rough grid pattern, seen in the majority of Iranian cities. A secondary configuration (found in other cities) is a radial pattern of streets converging in one or more central core areas of the city. Finally, there are cities such as Kirmānshāh, Sanandaj, Sārī, Burūjird, and Tabrīz whose streets do not follow any particular geometric order.

Factors Involved in the Shaping of Street Networks

Many reasons have been given for the apparently chaotic street patterns of Iranian (as well as other Middle Eastern) cities (e.g., Von Grunebaum 1955; Planhol 1959; English 1966a). Among them are the lack of motor vehicles, defense considerations, and the Islamic concept of privacy. The three most widely accepted explanations, however, have been the lack of a defined status for public versus private ownership in Islamic law; an inability on the part of civil authorities to impose a regular plan on the urban environment; and protection of the already existing streets from encroachment by private residences (Bonine 1979; Hakim 1986).

These explanations, however, have not been totally accepted by some recent scholars of Islamic cities (e.g., Frieden and Mann 1971; Wheatley 1976; Bonine 1979). Frieden and Mann, for example, in their discussion of traditional Iranian cities, speak of a rational circulation system (traffic network), which consists of the main street (the bazar) and the streets branching off it. The rationality for this system, in their view, is to be found in a mixture of geometry, the realities of land ownership, and topography (Frieden and Mann 1971: 14–15): ". . . there is reason to believe that bazaars and main kutchees [*sic*] follow old water courses, either qanats or streams. (In some cities even today many of the kutchees are built over the qanats and houses have stairways leading down to the water.) The kutchees which were water-related had to follow land contours as the water courses did. Off of this basic system, the plots of land for farming must have been geometrically arranged to rationalize ploughing and planting. The system of kutchees extended, in a roughly rectilinear pattern, to every house in the neighborhood."

Bonine (1979: 223) also mentions water courses and topography as definers of street patterns in Iranian cities: "Street systems in Iranian cities were constructed rationally given the environment and the pre-industrial economy. A grid pattern of main streets was established in conjunction with a system of channels used to irrigate agricultural land. The orientation of this network was determined by the need to arrange the rectangular fields and orchards to the slope of the land. Major streets, as well as many blind alleys, already existed within the field patterns before houses spread into these areas. Even the sizes and shapes of new suburban houses were governed by the preexisting system of fields and passageways."

These arguments about the role of topography and water in the development of street patterns are applicable to many traditional Iranian cities, particularly those located at the fringe of deserts. The case of Sabzivār is studied below.[8]

Streets of Sabzivār

Sabzivār is located on alluvial fans created by the deposition of sediments from seasonal streams draining the Ṭabas Mountains (part of the more extended Jughatāy [Chaghatāi] mountain range; see fig. 15). The Ṭabas Mountains are located north of Sabzivār, running from east to west. The city therefore slopes gently from north to south. The main water channels of the city were (and remain) a continuation of several major qanats that bring fresh water from the base of the Ṭabas Mountains to the city. They were in the form of open channels (*jūb*s) that ran in a north–south direction following the general slope of the land. The old major streets of the city, such as Iftikhār, Pāminār, Ḥammām-i Ḥakīm, and Niqābishk, followed the direction of the *jūb*s running along them. *Jūb*s also formed the center line of other smaller *kūchih*s and *bunbast*s.[9]

Branches coming off the main north–south irrigational channels ran both east and west. These branches formed a right angle at the point where they connected with the main channels or with one another. This may have been laid out in very early agricultural settlements to allow plots of farming lands located along the water channels to be geometrically arranged for a rational system of measuring, ploughing, and planting. Pathways were built along these water branches. The street map of Sabzivār indicates that some pathways, like Qāziān, Pādarakht, and Sabrīz, stretch along these major water branches.

By carefully observing the map of traditional Sabzivār, one notices that there are more major streets running north–south than east–west (see fig. 15). This is because the longest water channels of the city run in a north–south direction, and the longest streets of the city follow their courses. The branches coming off these major water channels are shorter in comparison: as a result, crossing streets and alleys following these branches are relatively shorter.

The conclusion from these observations is that it is no coincidence that the street pattern of Sabzivār displays a cardinal orientation. From the initial formation of the city, the streets and alleys

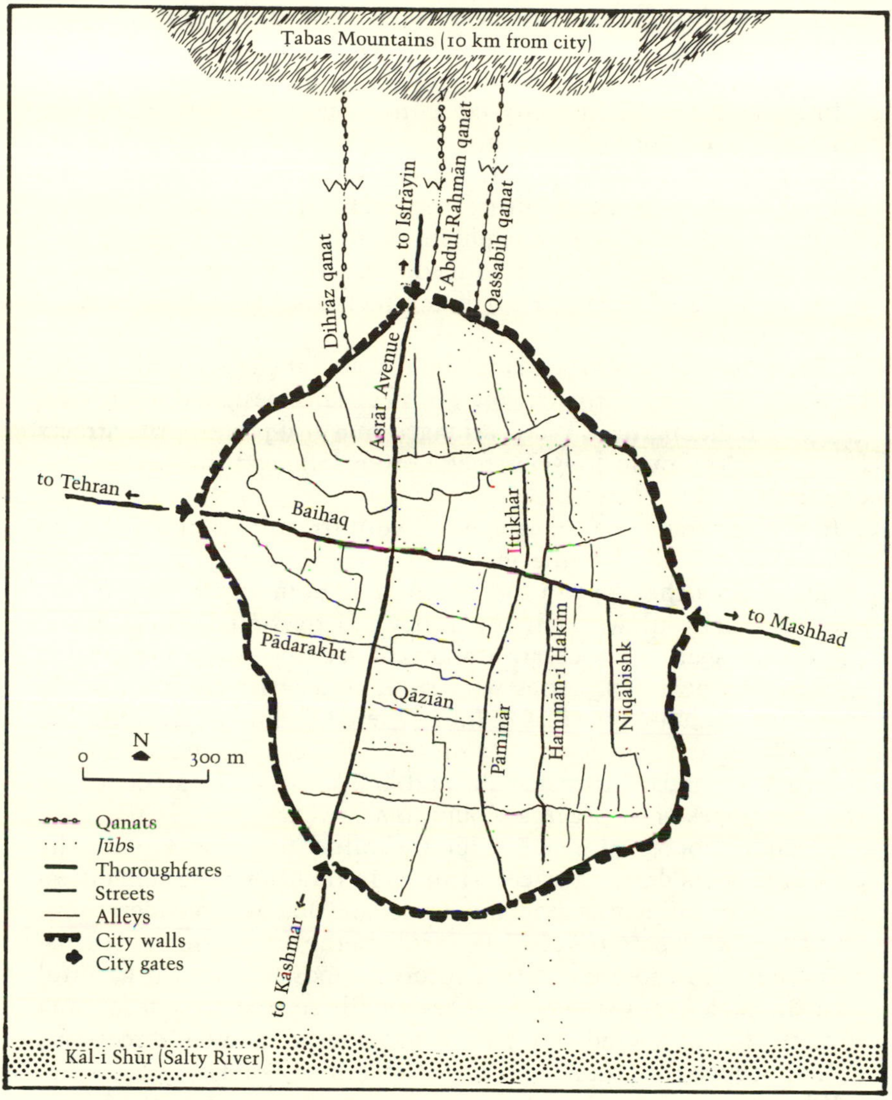

Figure 15. Street patterns in traditional Sabzivār; streets follow the direction of water courses.

have primarily followed the main water courses and their perpendicular branches. The water courses themselves have followed the slope of the land, in this case, in a north–south direction.

In some cases, when a city contains important cultural centers (such as the city of Mashhad with the shrine of Imām Rižā), streets usually follow a radial pattern of lanes (particularly around the shrine), converging at the cultural center. Even in grid pattern cities, an occasional radial pattern of public thoroughfares converging on a main cultural center can be noticed. This is seen in city plans of many traditional Iranian cities: their streets display both a grid and a radial pattern.

When the city was located on a relatively flat surface with a regular slope, the major streets were geometrically designed in either a grid or a radial pattern. When arranged in a grid pattern, the streets (especially the main longer streets) often followed the irrigational channels.

In places where the topography is very irregular, streets tend to follow no particular orientation or direction. Streets in such locales simply follow the slope of the terrain and go in any direction that the topography allows. Here proximity to irrigational channels and protection against floods are important factors in the location of streets (Bonine 1979). Cities with such street patterns are usually found in mountainous areas of Iran, where the annual precipitation is much higher than in the dry areas of the central regions of the country. Sanandaj, Kirmānshāh, and Burūjird, all located on the western slopes of the Zagros Mountains, are examples of this.

Although topography and water are influential, they are not the only categories defining street patterns in traditional Iranian cities; among other influences are wind, trade, and defense considerations. Prevailing wind patterns also play a role in the orientation of streets, particularly in those cities that receive winds laden with harmful dust. In such cities streets have been built so that they face away from the harmful winds and tend to meander in different directions, to help reduce the ground velocity of incoming winds.

While the concept of narrow winding streets is a rational cultural response of city dwellers to climate (i.e., sun and wind), it may also be related to defense considerations. The alleyways served to disorient strangers and to hinder the maneuverability of plundering horsemen in the confined quarters.

Finally, trade is an influential factor in the street layout. A major trade route passing through a settlement tends to lead to a linear growth of the main street (the bazar) along its course. For example, the bazar of Sabzivār is located on a stretch of the old trade route running east–west, connecting Mashhad to Tehran. Sometimes a bazar, or a segment of the trade route, also runs along a major water course. The influence of trade routes on the location and morphology of traditional Iranian cities is discussed in the following chapter.

The argument about what factors historically have been most responsible for the development of street forms and orientations in Iranian cities—as in many other parts of the world—remains open-ended. However, there are reasons to believe that topography and water—as Bonine (1979) and Frieden and Mann (1971) have also indicated—have played a major role in the development of street patterns in traditional Iranian cities.

Housing Patterns

Nearly all neighborhood buildings are private houses. Their general plan is an open rectangular courtyard, with rooms around two or more sides. By clustering together in a cell-like pattern, houses give a compact, organic appearance to the city. From the outside, they all look similar, having the same color, height, and even design. They are often built of sun-dried bricks, and, with few exceptions, have no outside decorations. Though similar in their outer appearance, houses do vary in internal design and architecture. Size and internal decoration are the indicators of the owner's taste and financial condition.

Houses are cell-like structures, attached to one another and sharing common walls.[10] In a typical house, one wall faces toward an alleyway, and the other three walls are joined to other houses. The house is entered through a small door set in the wall facing the alley. Entrances are often heavy wooden doors set into a niche, usually lower than the level of the *kūchih.* This difference in elevation is planned so that gravity flow feeds water running in *jūb*s along the *kūchih* into the house courtyard.

Plan of a Typical House. A typical house unit contains a central courtyard, usually having rooms arranged around it. Walls and roofs are thick and made of clay or bricks. The courtyard is situated below street level so that it is usually shaded. In addition to providing light for the rooms, the courtyard acts as a temperature moderator, retaining the colder night air to cool the house during the day. The tall surrounding walls of the courtyard also provide privacy for the residents. The center of the courtyard usually has a pool of water, often with a fountain in the middle, and gardens surrounding it (see figs. 16 and 17). The gardens contain flowers, vegetables, and fruit trees. Besides a comfortable microclimate produced by evaporative cooling, the pool and gardens create a pleasing aesthetic atmosphere.

Rooms are usually arranged around the courtyard in such a way that the summer rooms always face the north—away from the hot summer afternoon sun (especially in hot, arid regions). The shady, cool side of the house that faces away from the sun is known as the *nisār*. Summer rooms in their ideal form include the following components: a *tālār* or *ayvān* (no. 1 in fig. 18)—an open archway facing the courtyard; a *bād-gīr* (no. 2)—a ventilation wind tower or wind catcher; a *ḥauż-khānih* (no. 3)—a room usually beneath the *tālār* containing a little pool; and a *panj-darī* (no. 4)—literally meaning a room with five doors. The *panj-darī* is the largest room of the summer section and is used as a family living room.[11] Finally, there is the *zīr-zamīn* or *sardāb* (no. 5)—a large, deep basement also used as a family living area during the hotter hours of the day.

Although these elements are the main components of the summer area of the house, not all of them are necessarily found in any given house. The *tālār* and *zīr-zamīn* are found in most houses, regardless of their size or the financial status of their owners.

The *bād-gīr* is one of the most creative architectural structures found in Iranian settlements.[12] It resembles a chimney, eight to fifteen meters tall, the tallest being found in the houses of richer families. It is a very effective air conditioner, particularly common in arid regions of Iran where seasonal and daily patterns of winds are relatively fixed. The *bād-gīr* catches the prevailing summer winds and channels them down into the *tālār, zīr-zamīn,* or *ḥauż-khānih.* It operates by changing the temperature and thus the density of the air in and around the tower. As a result of the difference in pressure between the vent of the *bād-gīr* facing the prevailing wind and the vents facing away from the wind, the denser, cooled air sinks down through the tower while warmer air is drawn up from the space below and emitted from the tower to rejoin the ambient air stream (Bahadori 1978; Tavassoli 1983). The flow of air through different parts of the building can be controlled by opening and closing the doors of the tower and the doors of the rooms of the central hall.

When the air is channeled from the tower over the pool of the *ḥauż-khānih,* an efficient evaporative cooling system creates a pleasant atmosphere on hot summer afternoons. In the houses of richer families, there is usually a well tapping the water table or a qanat (which flows beneath the neighborhood) passing through a *zīr-zamīn* (basement) below the level of the house (fig. 18, nos. 5 and 6). If the house does not have a *ḥauż-khānih,* damp straw is put over the *bād-gīr*'s vents to cool, much like a "swamp cooler."

Figure 17. House in Sabzivār; summer rooms face north toward the courtyard.

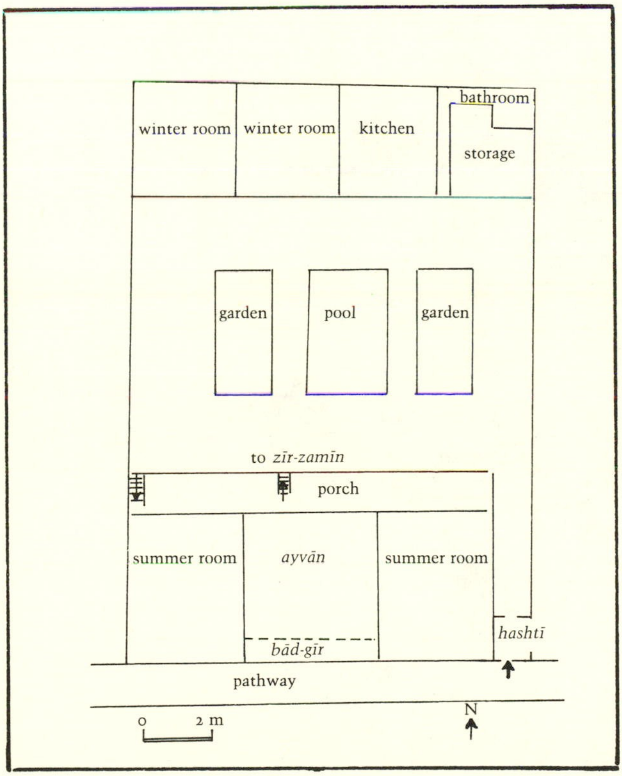

Figure 16. Plan of a typical house in arid regions.

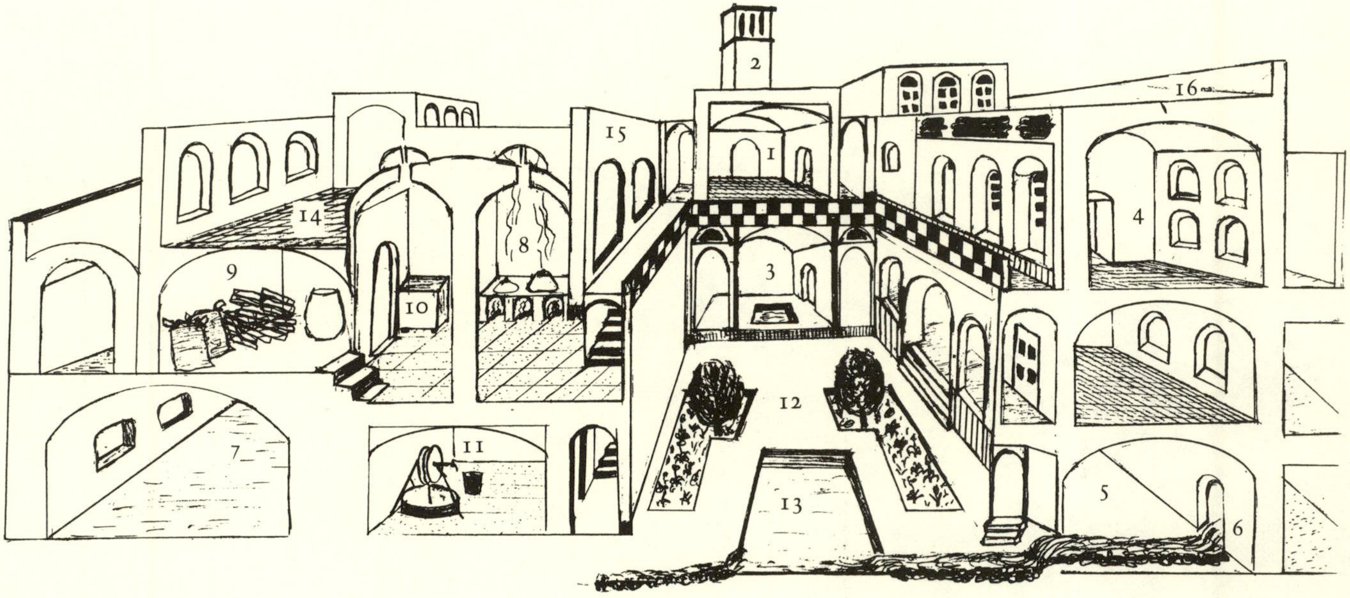

1. *Ayvān (tālār)*
2. *Bād-gīr* (wind catcher)
3. *Ḥauż-khānih*
4. Family living room
5. *Zīr-zamīn* (basement)
6. Qanat
7. Stable
8. Kitchen
9. Storage
10. Water tank
11. Water well
12. Courtyard garden
13. Pool
14. Guest courtyard
15. West-facing wall
16. Roof

Figure 18. Elements of an affluent family house in arid regions (based on Beazley and Haverson 1982).

The winter areas of the house are located opposite the summer areas, on the south side of the courtyard in order to expose it to the winter sun more effectively. Due to their location in relation to the sun, winter rooms are variably called *āftāb-rū* (facing sun) or *āftāb-gīr* (sun catchers). In many cities, such as Yazd, winter rooms face southwest, following the general street orientation of the city, instead of facing directly south. This direction, incidentally, corresponds to the *qiblih* (or *qibla*) direction of Mecca. However, the toilets in the bathrooms in traditional Iranian houses are always oriented in an east–west direction to avoid facing *qiblih* or having one's back toward it. In addition to the north- and south-facing rooms, there are also rooms located on the east or west side of the courtyard, used as kitchen, storage, and stable areas. Some are also used as regular living areas in various seasons.

In many parts of Iran, particularly the central region, ceilings are domed, made of mud or sun-dried bricks. These spherical or cylindrical domes allow the wind to cool their surfaces more easily and also minimize the intensity of radiation at any one point.

Flat roofs are used for sleeping surfaces during the summer nights. There the family can enjoy the cooler breezes not possible below, due to the nightly irradiation of heat from the walls that has been absorbed during the hot afternoon hours. The family's privacy is ensured by a small parapet, higher than standing eye-level, surrounding the edges of the roof. This wall also protects the family from excessive dust and wind (Bonine 1980).

Summary

Traditional Iranian cities have been built at the foothills of mountain chains on alluvial fans or in intermountain basins with access to water. They have been designed in such a way as to minimize the effects of heat, wind, and dust and to harness natural forces to create better living conditions for their inhabitants. The city's peculiar morphology reduces undesirable climatic stresses, such as intense radiation and strong, harmful, dusty winds. At the same time it utilizes available natural resources to provide various means of comfort, such as shaded private and public spaces and water-cooled residential houses. In short, contrary to the tendencies of present planners, the builders of these traditional cities, in the process of forming the physical urban design, have always worked with, not against, the forces of nature.

CHAPTER THREE

TRADE, HISTORICAL EVENTS, AND THE CITY

THE RELATIONSHIP BETWEEN the location of cities and the ancient trade routes and the role that political leaders have played historically in the formation and development of Iranian cities are examined in this chapter. The bazar as the heart of the traditional Iranian city and its morphology and function as the main urban core are discussed.

Five main questions are dealt with here.

1. What roles have trade routes played in the formation of early Iranian cities?
2. What was the role of kings and other powerful leaders in the development and form of Iranian cities?
3. How did the small agricultural settlements develop into commercial towns and cities?
4. How was the bazar developed, and why did it become the core of the city?
5. How does the bazar function within a traditional Iranian city?

City Sites and Trade Routes

Since antiquity, nearly all of the major Iranian cities have been located along the major trade routes that, interestingly enough, follow the desert fringe. The main east–west route was commercial and military and for the most part followed the southern foothills of the Alburz Mountains (see fig. 19). It was part of the famous Silk Route (*jāddih-yi abrīsham*), the most important commercial route of the ancient world, covering over ten thousand kilometers, from China to Syria. Starting in the northern and western boundaries of China, and passing through present Soviet Central Asia, this route crossed the Iranian Plateau and, passing Mesopotamia, continued through Syria to the port of Antioch on the Mediterranean.[1]

Within the Iranian Plateau, the Silk Route connected some major ancient cities such as Nīshāpūr, Rey, Qazvīn, and Tabrīz. Some major capitals of Iran, since the time of the Median Empire in the seventh century B.C., have been located along this route. Among them are Dāmghān, Ecbatana (present Hamadān), Qazvīn, Rey, and the current capital of the country, Tehran (fig. 19).

The other major ancient route was the Royal (Imperial) Achaemenid Road (*jāddih-yi shāhanshāhī*), which stretched over a distance of 2,500 kilometers.[2] It connected Persepolis (the summer capital of the Achaemenids) to Susa (their winter capital) and, continuing northwest, reached Sardis, the capital of Lydia (western Anatolia). According to Herodotus, there were 111 *kārvānsarāy*s (or *caravanserai*s: houses for caravans) located along this road between Sardis and Susa (Komroff 1928: 282–283).[3]

Another major north–south route connected the city of Rey to Iṣfahān; from there it continued through Shīrāz all the way to the Persian Gulf. The ancient capitals of Eṣpahān (present Iṣfahān), Pasargadae, and Persepolis were located along this route (Siroux 1949). A large number of medieval and ancient Iranian cities are found near or at the site of modern cities along the ancient trade routes. These cities are scattered along the foothills of the high mountain chains in the desert fringe or in intermountain basins where water and arable lands were available.

It is interesting to note that, although the Caspian lowlands contain many large, important cities today, until the present century none of these cities had been a main capital or had played a major political or economical role during the course of Iranian history. The reasons for this are the physical nature of the terrain and the lack of any major roads in the area. As a result of the high, rocky mountains, heavy rains, and lush forests, no major road passed through the area until recent times. The few existing trail-like routes were continuously flooded by rivers and created many problems for travelers. Therefore, caravans avoided traveling through the region (Siroux 1949).

This area also has a hot, humid climate, especially during the summer. This creates an environment that fosters the spread of malaria and similar diseases. While—unlike the Central Plateau—this region had an annual surplus of water, the unfavorable climatic conditions, rugged terrain, and lush forests hindered the building of trade routes that could have resulted in the establishment of major commercial cities here.

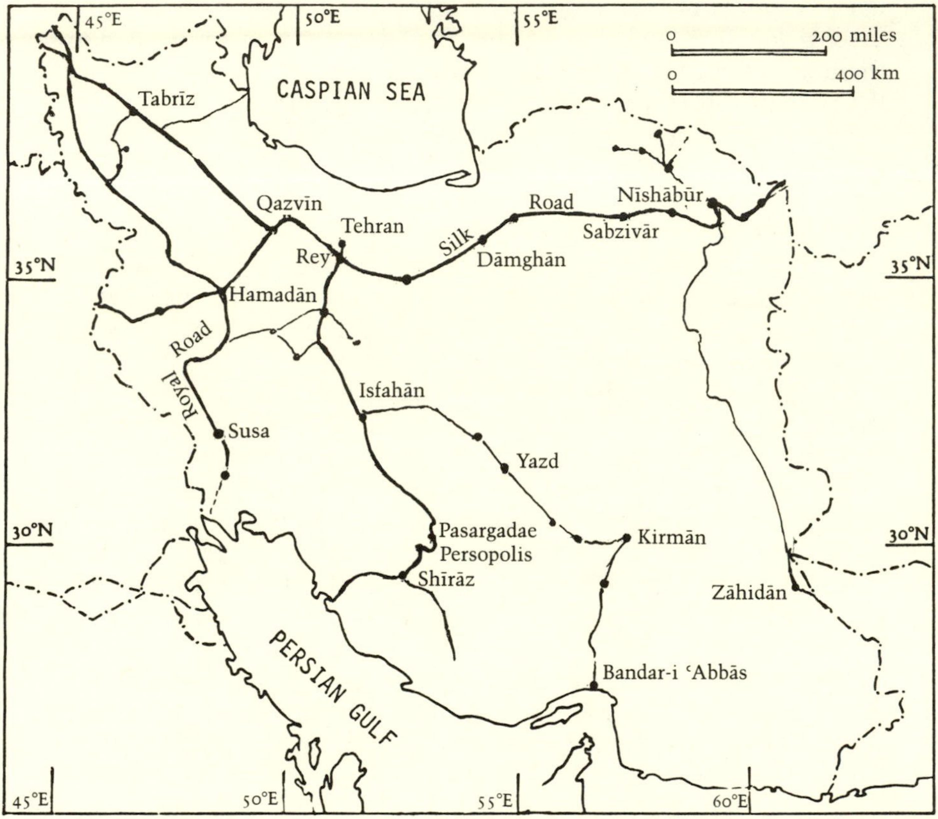

Figure 19. The old Iranian trade routes (adapted from 1971 *Atlas of Iran*).

Political decisions also played an important role in the selection of city sites. Many kings and princes built their own cities and left their marks on Iranian townscapes. Those cities that were located on the better sites survive today, while those not favorably located have been abandoned (or never grew into major settlements). Among the latter is the city of Sulṭānīyyih, built to serve as the capital of Oljiytu (reigned 1304–1316), a powerful king of the Mongol dynasty

(1220–1375). The city was built near the present city of Zanjān; people from the vicinity and from other towns were moved into this new city. The king built many important buildings, and the city became popular during his reign (Ashraf 1974).

After Oljiytu's death and the collapse of his dynasty, the city failed to survive. People deserted the city and it gradually deteriorated into an insignificant settlement. Unlike other Iranian cities, it was built in an area without adequate water and arable hinterlands and was isolated from major trade routes. Although it still reflects its former glory in the magnificent temple of its founder Oljiytu (170 feet above the ground), today the small settlement of Sulṭānīyyih languishes. It is a good example of a city built on an inadequate site.

Religious factors also influenced the formation of some Iranian cities. The best examples of cities built for religious reasons are Mashhad and Qum. Mashhad was formed around the shrine of Imām Riżā (Eighth Shiʿite Muslim *Imām*) who lived during the early ninth century A.D. It gradually developed into a progressively larger city; today it is the second largest Iranian city. Qum was formed at about the same time. Built around the shrine of Maʿṣūmih, the sister of Imām Riżā, it is presently the most significant center for religious studies in Iran.

One important note about these two cities is that Mashhad is located in an intermountain basin along the east–west trade route and Qum is located at the desert fringe south of Tehran, along the north–south trade route. Both contain arable hinterlands and are irrigated by qanats. In addition, Mashhad is partly irrigated by the Kashaf-Rūd, which originates in the highlands of the Alburz Mountains. This river passes through Khurāsān Province and then joins the Harī-Rūd in Afghanistan. The importance of religion in the formation and development of cities is discussed in the next chapter.

Generally speaking, locations of Iranian cities have been determined by such factors as physical geography, presence of trade routes, and military, cultural, political, and religious considerations. However, in Iran, as in many other parts of the world, cities traditionally have been built in areas with an available source of water and relatively arable hinterland.

Formation and Development of Cities

With the specialization of areas of the ancient Middle East in the production of various goods, trading activities began to flourish. Caravans were the means of distribution of goods to consumers living in different places. To provide a resting place for the members

Figure 20. Kārvānsarāy near Tehran along the ancient Silk Road; a new highway now follows the major course of the old route.

Figure 21. Kārvānsarāy near Sabzivār along the ancient Silk Road.

of the caravan (hereafter referred to as *kārvānīs*) and to provide protection for the trade goods, *kārvānsarāys* (the Persian term for caravan houses) were developed (for a further description of *kārvānsarāys*, see appendix B). Figure 20 shows an old *kārvānsarāy* along the Silk Road, near Tehran. Another *kārvānsarāy* (from the seventeenth century) along the same road in ʿAbbās-ābād, near Sabzivār, is seen in figure 21. The following section demonstrates how a small agricultural settlement along a major trade route could gradually have grown into a commercial town.

Kārvānsarāys were usually built in small agricultural settlements along the trade routes, where *kārvānīs* could be provided with a supply of water and food. Functioning as commercial nodes, the settlements containing *kārvānsarāys* attracted ever larger numbers of traders and laborers from neighboring areas. The major street of these settlements, along which the *kārvānsarāys* were built, began to function as a main market and center for trade. Several public buildings were added to provide for the other needs of the *kārvānīs*. As more shops were built along this street, it became the settlement's major core and trade center and gradually evolved into a linear bazar. To protect the users from heat and rain, this bazar became first partially and later totally covered. As more and more traders were attracted to these growing settlements, more *kārvānsarāys* were built along the bazar. (The larger *kārvānsarāys* capable of unloading caravans' pack animals were built outside the covered bazar, usually near the edges of the settlement.)

As the population grew, the pattern of land use within the settlement usually began to change. More shops were attracted to the *kārvānsarāy*'s vicinity along the bazar, and the agricultural lands gradually gave way to other residential and commercial uses. As the settlement grew larger, there was a need for more services. As a result of this, another qanat was built, and more public buildings were constructed. To provide security and defense, a governmental seat was established and a wall was erected around the settlement to provide protection and defense. Through this sequence of events the settlement gradually evolved into a commercial town. Figure 22 shows the gradual development of a small agricultural settlement along a major trade route into a commercial city.

The bazar was the center of the city; its growth and decline were interrelated with the growth and decline of the city itself. Generally, the growth of the bazar was organic, a response both to the needs of a growing population and to the needs of a flourishing trade. The bazar expanded along the main city axes and sometimes developed additional linear branches along streets situated at right angles to them.

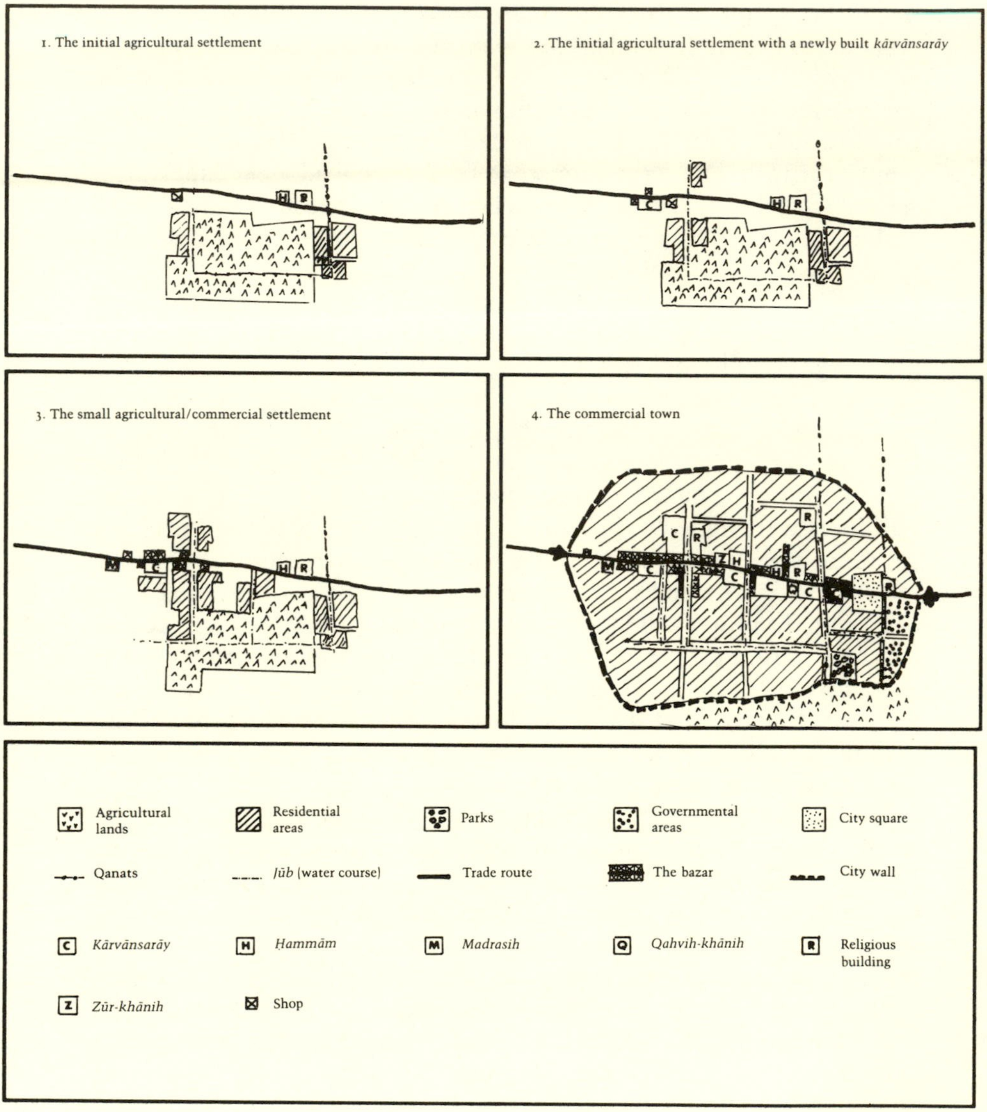

Figure 22. Schematic evolution of a commercial city along a trade route.

With the growth of bazars came the development of residential areas, which were always concentrated around the bazar and within the city walls. This pattern of growth, with focus on the bazar, emphasized the bazar's importance as the economic and sociocultural center of the city.

The growth of the bazar (and the city), however, was not always directly linked to population growth. In many cases, important political leaders brought changes to cities by rebuilding some older parts of the existing bazar, adding new parts, or building a completely different one in another section of the city. When an entirely new bazar was built, the corẹ of the city gradually shifted from its former location to the site of the new bazar. For example, in Iṣfahān, after the construction of a new bazar north of the Shah's Square by Shah ʿAbbās I (reigned 1587–1629), the core of the city gradually shifted from the area of the old bazar (around the Friday Mosque) to the site of this new bazar (see Gaube 1979: 87–92). In many Iranian bazars, one can easily distinguish the portions added by kings or other leaders by their unique geometric designs and harmonious spatial arrangements. The bazars and monuments seen in Iṣfahān, Shīrāz, Tabrīz, Qazvīn, Kirmān, Mashhad, and Tehran are good examples of the creativity of their various builders, who skillfully blended design, architecture, and spatial arrangement.

Iṣfahān is a particularly good example of royal influence in Iranian city planning. The bazar and many other important structures were developed under the reign of Shah-ʿAbbās I, the most popular king of the Safavid Dynasty. In 1597, when Shah ʿAbbās moved his capital from Qazvīn to Iṣfahān, the city was in a deteriorated state. As king of a vast empire, this shah wanted to develop his new capital into a great city, to rival the majestic city of Istanbul (Constantinople), the capital of the Ottoman Empire, and other great contemporary European cities. So, with the help of Sheikh Bahāʾī, his engineer and city planner, Shah ʿAbbās built large public squares (*maydān*s) and avenues wide enough to accommodate the royal coaches. These were also well suited for conducting military shows. He also built many mosques and *madrasih*s to consolidate Shiʿism (which had become the official religion of Iran under the religious rule of his great grandfather, Shah Ismāʿīl) as the main religion of the country. As a result of his great interest in trade, Shah ʿAbbās also modified the old bazar in Iṣfahān and added new branches with magnificent structures such as the shah's *kārvānsarāy* and others (Hunarfar 1978; Gaube 1979).

Figure 23 illustrates the bazar of Iṣfahān and related public buildings. The great Maydān-i Shāh (Shah's Square), also known as Naqsh-i Jahān (Image of the World), is seen at the center of the figure. To the

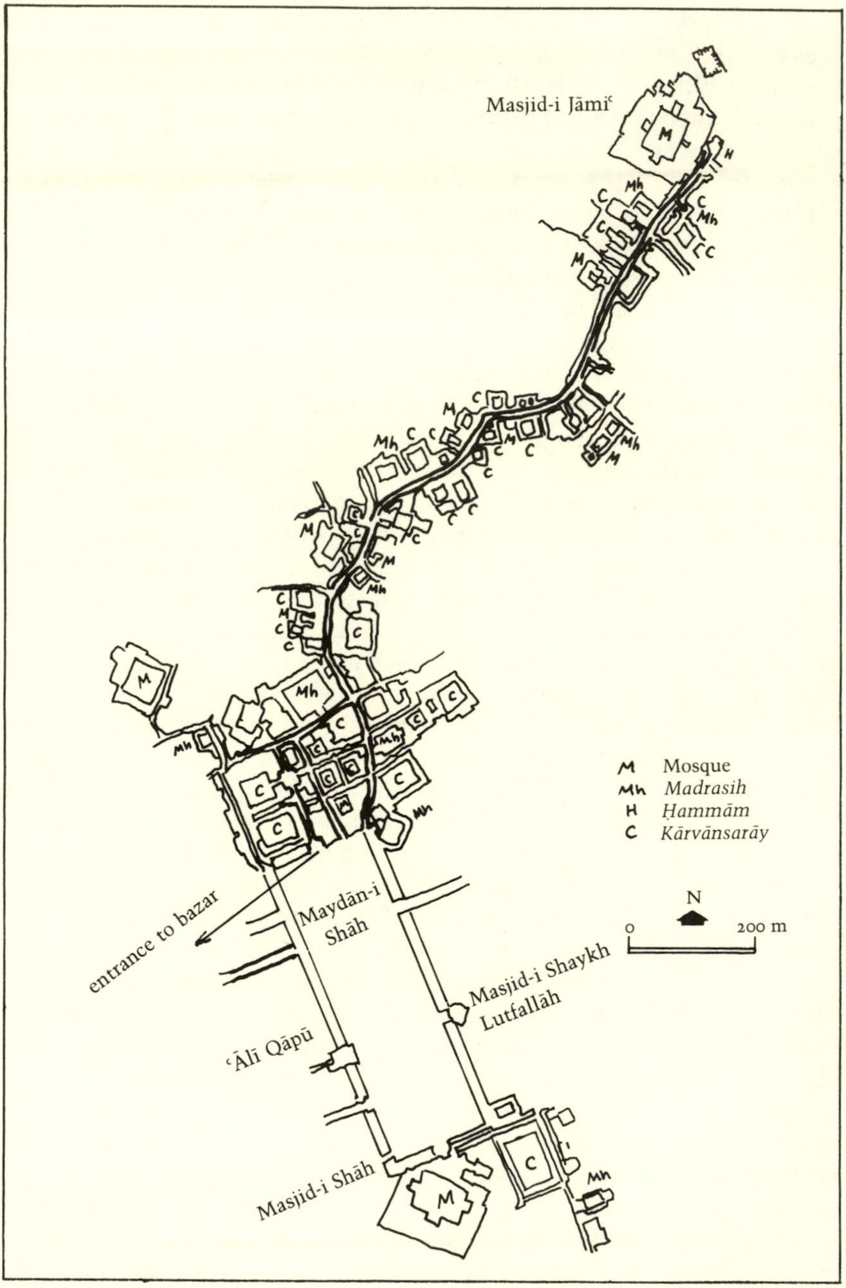

Figure 23. Bazar of Iṣfahān (adapted from Ardalan and Bakhtiar 1979 and Tavassoli 1982).

right of the *maydān* is the Masjid-i Shaykh Lutfullāh (a Mosque built by Shah ʿAbbās I, named after his father-in-law), and to its left is ʿĀlī Qāpū, a palace in which Shah ʿAbbās I resided. To the south of the *maydān* is the Masjid-i Shāh (or Shah's Mosque, also built by Shah ʿAbbās); to the north of the *maydān* is the arched entrance to the great bazar of Iṣfahān. The bazar runs over a mile to the north, within the city, and leads to the Masjid-i Jāmiʿ (Congregational Mosque).

Shīrāz is another example of the importance of a leader's taste and decisions in the development of the spatial pattern and morphology of Iranian cities. It flourished under the reign of Karīm Khān (1759–1779), the founder of the Zand Dynasty (Clarke 1966). Karīm Khān added many new structures to the city. Among them are the present Bāzār-i Vakīl, Arg-i Karīm-khānī (royal residence), and a long, wide avenue called Bulvār-i Karīm Khān i Zand (Karīm Khān Zand Boulevard). Ruled by kings for over twenty-five hundred years, many other Iranian cities display the vivid impact of powerful individuals on their morphology.

The Bazar: The Core of the City

The bazar is the heart of the traditional Iranian city. Without it, a settlement is not considered a city (Falamaki 1977). The bazar usually forms all or part of the main street that connects the two main entrance gates located at either end of the walled city. While the bazar is the focus of public life as the major commercial center, it is also the center of social, cultural, recreational, religious, and political activities. By containing buildings such as mosques, shrines, religious schools, hotels, bathhouses, sport clubs, and *ḥusaynīyyih*s (places of mourning), the bazar functions as a complete integrated body. Structurally, it is usually covered by a roof of vaulted brickwork.

Morphology of the Bazar

The main linear bazar (*bāzār-i buzurg*) usually begins at the major *maydān* (square) of the city and often advances through two or more of the most important cultural centers. The main bazar forms the major thoroughfare within the city; its path, extending from opposite ends of the square, eventually connects the main city gates at either end of the city.

A good example of the typical Iranian bazar is the one of Iṣfahān, shown in figure 23. The bazar of Iṣfahān stretches throughout the city and connects the mosque, *kārvānsarāy*s, and other major buildings. The main bazar starts at the famous Maydān-i Shāh (Shah's Square) and leads to the Masjid-i Jāmiʿ (Congregational Mosque) in the north, a distance of over a mile. The bazar reaches both the northern and southern gates and is the main focus of the city. Its role as the major north-south axis of Iṣfahān is evident: it encompasses the primary commercial, religious, and governmental areas of the city.[4]

The *maydān* consists of two royal mosques to the south and east and a royal palace to the west, which were all built during the sixteenth century. A line of earthen mounds indicates the course of the bazar stretched underneath. The mounds are a mixture of sun-dried mud and straw and cover the bazar's brick vaulted ceiling. Beneath the vaults, the tunnel-like bazar is dark and cool, lit only by shafts of sunlight from the small hole cut in each mound for this purpose (fig. 24). The spatial pattern and morphology of the bazar of Iṣfahān

Figure 24. Rāstih-bāzār in Iṣfahān; the fact that the level floor of the bazar is lower than the neighboring areas causes better air circulation.

are similar to those of other traditional Iranian bazars. For example, in the city of Qazvīn the bazar (dating from the sixteenth century) was the main north–south axis of that city and connected the palace and the Friday Mosque (Beaudouin and Pope 1967).

The collected buildings of the main bazar and the other major and minor branches that form the traditional Iranian bazar are called the *majmūʿi-yi bāzār* or bazar complex. This traditional bazar complex is a complex of parallel and intersecting galleries (each gallery is known as a *rāstih-bāzār,* a segment of the bazar that is lined with shops on both sides along its course). These galleries are covered either with vaulted brickwork roofs or with wooden roofs, depending on the material available in the region. Vaulted brickwork roofs are used mainly in the hot and arid or cold mountainous regions of the country. Each roof contains a central opening, both to provide lighting to the room underneath and for ventilation purposes.

Shops are nestled into spaces between roof-supporting buttresses and are built along each side of the gallery, optimally, on an elevated platform fifty to a hundred centimeters above the floor of the central passageway. This elevation is necessary to protect the shopkeepers and their customers from the constant dust created by passing pack animals and from the mud that forms on the floor of the passageway during the rainy season. Between the shops are entrances to the large, unroofed spaces that form the courtyards of *kārvānsarāy*s, or courtyards of other public buildings such as *madrasih*s, *ḥusaynīyyih*s, and mosques. The morphology of Iranian bazars has been well described by Kenneth Browne (Browne and Cantacuzino 1976: 260) in his description of the bazar of Iṣfahān:

> The primary movement system of the bazaar forms a central linear circulation space, splendidly domed throughout its length, parallel to which on both sides run the small and regular dependent spaces of the shops. Between them, at frequent intervals, arched entrances lead to the larger spaces—caravanserais, colleges,[5] bath houses, shrines, mosques and stores, all tightly connected to the central spine yet each a separate, self-contained world. Each has its individual character—the "hammams," or baths, enclosed, steamy, restful; the caravanserais each a busy square varying greatly in size and open to the sky and generally containing a central pool and trees with merchants' accommodation ranged round the perimeter. The mosques, also with courts open to the air, provide havens of tranquillity and contemplation, a step away from the noisy barter of the tunnel-like bazaar.

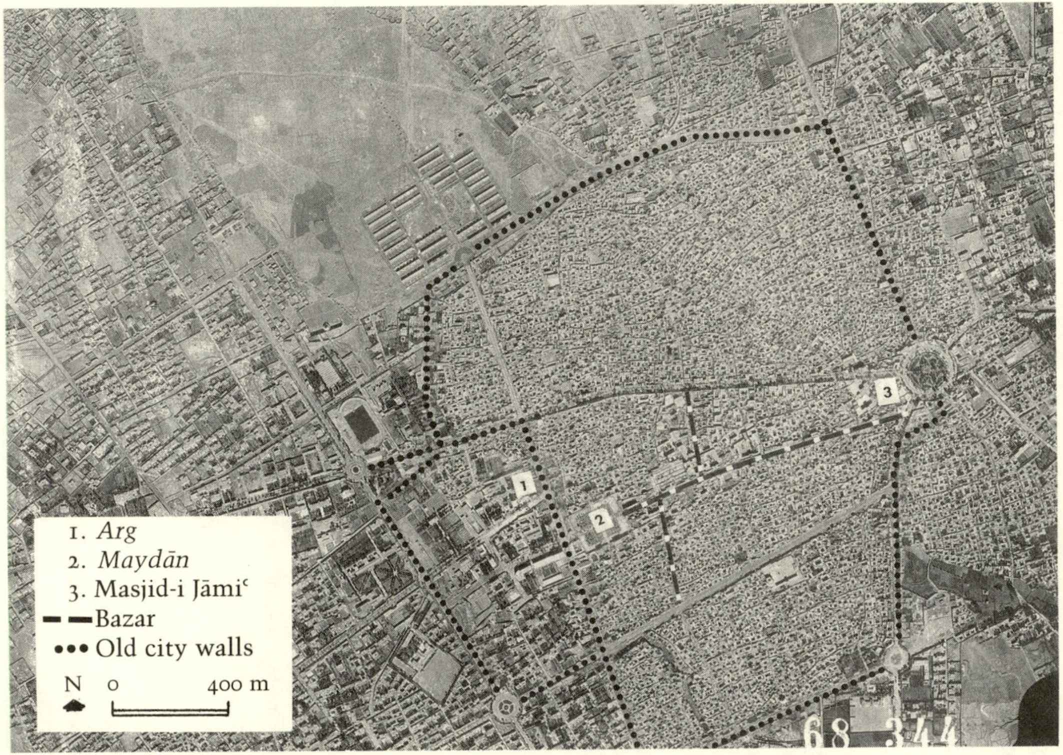

Figure 25. Traditional city of Kirmān; the bazar, with its associated public buildings, forms the core of the city (1956 aerial photograph, National Cartographic Center, Iran; original scale 1 : 20,000).

Another good example of the Iranian bazar is the one in Kirmān. Figure 25 shows the bazar of Kirmān and its loction within the city. The bazar, at its western end, begins at the Maydān-i Arg (the citadel square) and continues as the major thoroughfare of the city until it ends at the Masjid-i Jāmiᶜ (Congregational Mosque) to the east. Extending over half a mile throughout the heart of the city, the bazar connects the eastern and western entrance gates of the city. Along its course, the main bazar of Kirmān is intersected by other perpendicular branches. Most of these branches, like the main bazar itself, are covered by a roof of vaulted brickwork.[6] The bazar complex of Kirmān includes many shops, *kārvānsarāy*s, and other commercial buildings. It also includes many public buildings such as mosques, *madrasih*s, *ḥusaynīyyih*s, *ḥammām*s (bathhouses), and *āb-anbār*s (water cisterns).

Although the bazars of larger cities, such as Iṣfahān and Kirmān, outshine those of smaller Iranian cities in their architectural design and elegance, their general layout and morphology, in principle, are similar to those of smaller cities such as Sabzivār.[7]

Until about 1920, the main bazar of the city of Sabzivār was also its main east–west street and connected the two most important gates of the city, Darvāzih-yi Nishābūr (Nishābūr Gate) to the east, and Darvāzih-yi Irāq to the west. The main bazar started at the main *maydān* (square), facing the Nishābūr Gate, and connected the Masjid-i Pāminār (the mosque at the foot of the minaret), the Masjid-i Jāmiᶜ, and the Imāmzādih Yaḥyā (the holy shrine of Yaḥyā, one of the Shiᶜite saints). A north–south bazar intersected the main bazar to the west of the Imāmzādih Yaḥyā; the continuation of this bazar connected the *arg* (city citadel) to the Imāmzādih Yaḥyā. Figure 26 shows the traditional city of Sabzivār and its bazar.[8]

Today the wide avenue of Baihaq (Beihaq) has replaced the old bazar. However, there are still many relics of the old bazar left to be seen, like its *ḥammām*s (public baths), *masjid*s (mosques), *madrasih*s (religious schools), and some *bāzārchih*s (branches of the old bazar). The main north–south running branch of the old bazar still accounts for one of the major centers of commerce in the city. It is linear, parallel to the southern half of Asrār Avenue, which connects the two other city gates, Darvāzih-yi Arg (Citadel Gate) to the north and Darvāzih-yi Sabrīz to the south. This bazar, unlike the main old bazar, which was covered by a vaulted roof, now has a metal roof that contrasts sharply with the surrounding vaulted roofs. The floor level of this bazar is also more than one meter lower than the neighboring street. Although this bazar does not include the elegant and expensive shops, such as those found in new shop-

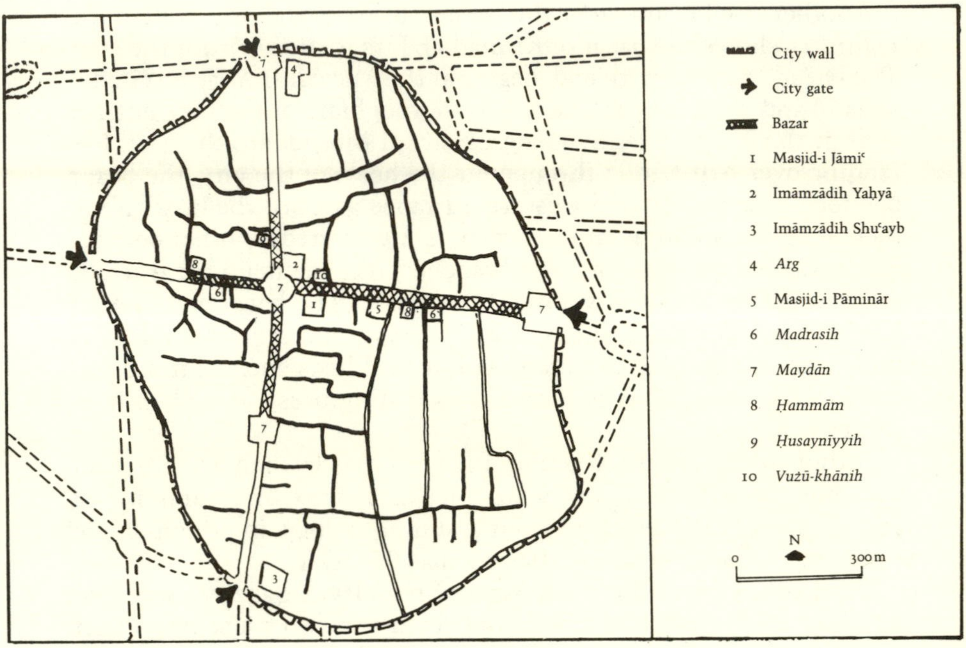

Figure 26. Traditional city of Sabzivār.

ping areas along major streets, its natural air currents and cozy atmosphere still make it a favorite place for shopping or browsing—especially during the hot summer days in Sabzivār. Figures 27, 28, and 29 illustrate the bazar and its configuration within the city.

In traditional Iranian cities, the bazar is surrounded by compact and roughly circular areas of residential housing. The pattern of movement in the city through the bazar and its outlying streets is discussed in chapter 2. The organization of the residential neighborhoods is discussed in the next chapter.

Iranian bazars differ, depending upon their dates of formation, their historical development, and their spheres of influence. For example, a bazar in a large city (such as a former capital or a major commercial node) differs from a bazar in a small city that has never been commercially important on a national or international level. Because of its greater sphere of influence, a bazar in a capital city or any other large city must be able to satisfy a greater number of customers with different tastes and varied demands. The bazar must naturally be larger, including both more shops dealing with a greater

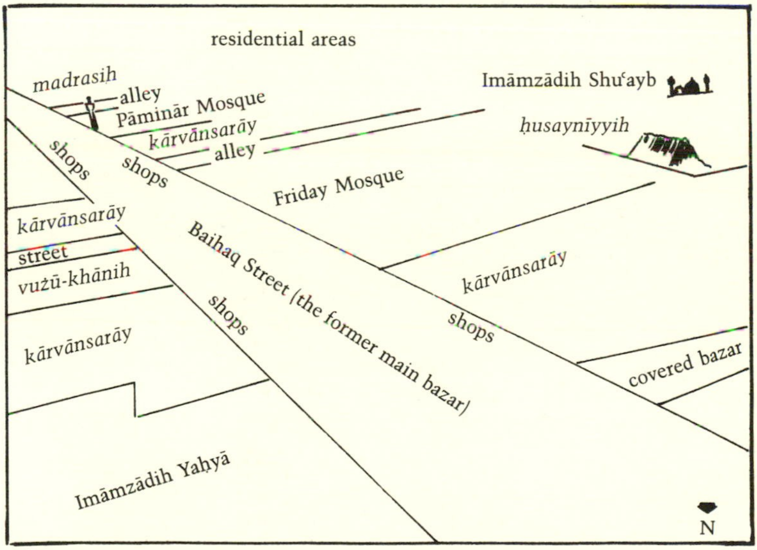

Figure 27. Sabzivār: the main street and associated elements; the main bazar of the traditional city has been deroofed and widened to form the major street of the modern city.

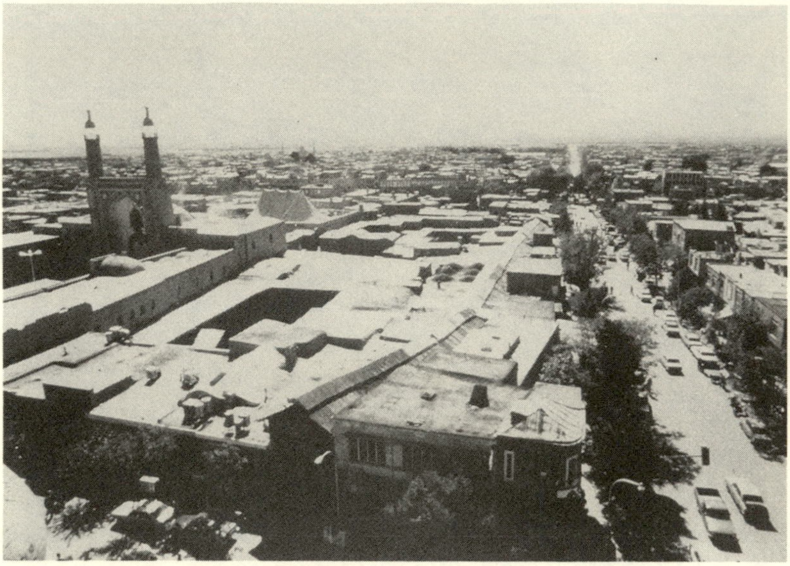

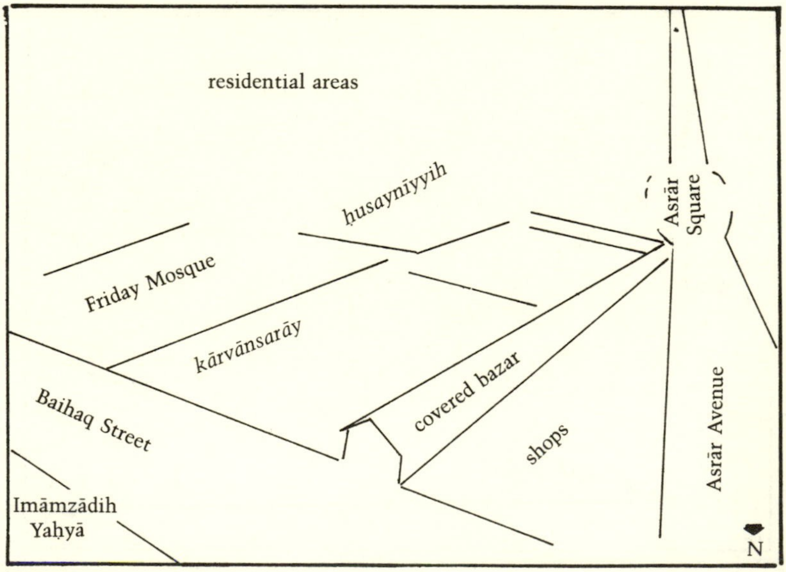

Figure 28. Sabzivār: the city center; the present bazar was a major branch of the main bazar; the original domed roof has been replaced by a metallic one.

A

B

Figure 29. The contemporary bazar of Sabzivār: A, entrance to the bazar; B, inside the bazar.

variety of goods and more *rāstih-bāzār*s allocated to different types of trade. It must also contain more public buildings (mosques, *madrasih*s, etc.) and in some cases, such as the bazar of Tehran, churches and synagogues.[9] In contrast, the small bazars such as that of Sabzivār, as a result of their smaller spheres of influence and limited numbers of customers, are much smaller in size. With reduced customer demand for less essential goods, the smaller bazars instead concentrate on trading local goods that satisfy the basic needs of the inhabitants of the city and its immediate surroundings.

The morphology of traditional Iranian bazars, to a great extent, is related to the functional characteristics of the bazar. For example, various *rāstih-bāzār*s are allocated to different commercial activities.

Function of the Bazar

Trade was the primary activity within the bazar. In Iran, as in many other parts of the Middle East, different types of trades and crafts were spatially segregated; people of the same profession occupied their own particular *rāstih-bāzār.* Even now, in existing traditional bazars, one can see *rāstih-bāzār*s organized into bazars of coppersmiths, blacksmiths, goldsmiths, and shoemakers. However, certain shops such as bakeries, groceries, and restaurants have always been sprinkled throughout the different linear bazars. They also existed outside of the bazar complex in the various centers of residential areas.

People of similar crafts or trades were usually organized into a single guild-group, headed by one or two *ustād*s (masters of the guilds). Each group had its own professional name, like the Ṣinf-i Kaffāsh-hā or shoemakers' guild (*ṣinf* is guild in Persian). Leaders of each group represented their members in the *hay'at-i aṣnāf* (the city-wide organization of all *ṣinf*s) and worked closely with government agents when dealing with security, taxation, and so forth. Duties of *ustād*s included collecting taxes according to each member's income; setting prices; controlling the quality of goods; granting permission to open new shops; organizing religious and cultural activities; and participating in political activities.

Many reasons can be given for the development of segregated professions in Iranian as well as other Middle Eastern bazars. The taxation system practiced by the ruling powers was simplified when people of similar crafts or trades gathered along the same *rāstih-bāzār.* This gave the government's taxing agents a better estimate of the bazar members' incomes when the incomes of neighboring shopkeepers could be compared (Bonine 1981). The unloading of pack animals of the arriving caravans was made easier: the goods could be unloaded in the *kārvānsarāys* located in specific *rāstih-bāzārs* that specialized in that merchandise. The hereditary system of trade and craftsmanship within the bazar led to the allocation of certain professions to certain families; retaining the traditional location of the business was encouraged among the heirs as a mark of distinction (Von Grunebaum 1955; English 1966a; Bonine 1981). The security process was more effective: it was much easier for the bazar's guards to protect jewelry, for example, when all of the jewelry shops were lined up on either side of a single *rāstih-bāzār*.

The most probable reason for the continued acceptance of the segregated system was its sheer practicality. One can understand the rationale behind this system when considering the benefits gained by shopkeepers as well as customers through this kind of spatial organization. The concentration of similar craftsmen and traders within a single bazar led to constant interaction, allowing for the exchange of professional, political, and religious ideas. This communication usually reduced the possibility of alienation and enhanced the degree of unification among the members of a particular profession.[10]

The customer also benefited from this system to a great extent, being given a wide choice of similar goods and at the same time being able to compare the different levels of quality and price offered. This system itself set an inescapable price control throughout the bazar and minimized any possible fraud by shopkeepers. The system also saved the time and energy of the shoppers by providing them with many different commodities in one location rather than many locations scattered throughout the city.

Bazars, particularly in large cities, functioned as the sites for the exchange of goods between caravan merchants and local bazar merchants. The caravan merchants, who often were involved in national as well as international trade, either sold their goods directly to the local merchants or used the merchants as middlemen or broker agents. The caravan merchants also bought the local merchandise through the local merchants and sold it in the bazars of other cities or countries.

The local bazar merchants also regulated the production of local commodities. They contracted with local workers who produced marketable goods both for the local bazar and for export. Goods such as carpets and clothing were produced on commission for bazar merchants by artisans in outlying residential areas or villages.

Traditional Iranian bazars have been compared to the city squares of preindustrial European cities. Falamaki (1977: 103) compares the traditional Iranian bazars to the city squares of preindustrial France, Italy, and other European countries. In his discussion of the relationship between the bazar and the city square, he indicates that the bazar in Iran shared the functional quality of the European city square as a gathering place for citizens. In the bazar, as in the city square, people played a major role in economic and administrative decisions related to the city. The bazar, he believes, was actually an alternative to the power of the ruling class. For example, if an unpopular decision or law was made by those with political power, the bazar immediately became the site of heated discussion and vehement protest.

According to Falamaki, the functioning of the economic, social, religious, and cultural centers within the single institution of the bazar was a phenomenon common to Iranian cities. The administrative affairs of the city were conducted in spaces provided for that purpose in the bazar. Najmi (1983) describes how, in olden days in the city of Tehran, the *dārūghih* (or *dārūgha,* the chief of police of a traditional Iranian city) had his regular headquarters in one of the main *chahār sūq*s (the domed, large spaces created at the intersection of two main *rāstih-bāzār*s, also called *chahār sūs*) and administered the affairs of the bazar and the city from his bazar headquarters.

There was always a well-defined alliance between the members of the bazar (*bāzārī*s) and the *ʿulamā* (religious leaders). In many instances, the *ʿulamā* came from the ranks of the *bāzārī*s. *Bāzārī*s were usually educated in *maktab*s (elementary schools), and *madrasih*s, and the bazar lent itself to the discussion of religious matters, which were tightly intertwined with politics and the economy. A shopkeeper who was also known for his high degree of piety and religiosity would attract the highest number of customers and was usually a *hājī* (a title for one who has made the pilgrimage to Mecca).

*Bāzārī*s have tended to support the religious establishments financially and morally throughout Iran's Islamic history. They also have often become actively involved in the opposition to those centralized governments that (in the *bāzārī*s' view) neglect traditional religious values. Good examples of *bāzārī*s' involvement in politics were seen both during the constitutional movement of the early twentieth century and during the Revolution of 1979. The closure of their shops by the Tehran *bāzārī*s during the Revolution as a show of opposition to the shah's regime was very effective and contributed to the establishment of the present Islamic Republic of Iran.[11]

In summary, the bazar was clearly the heart of the traditional Iranian city and served as its major thoroughfare. Containing the major public buildings, it functioned as a completely integrated body. The bazar was the center not only of commerce, but also of social, cultural, religious, and political activities. The following chapter studies these activities and their representative structures within the traditional city.

CHAPTER FOUR

RELIGION, SOCIOPOLITICAL STRUCTURES, AND THE CITY

THIS CHAPTER BEGINS with a brief overview of pre-Islamic religions of Iran and their impact on the city morphology and then elaborates on Islamic influences. The location, form, and functions of the mosque as a major element of an Iranian city are examined, as well as the urban requirements of Shiʿite Islam and spatial patterns within the city. This chapter also briefly explores the impact of the sociopolitical structures of Iran on the city morphology and related urban structures and examines the division of residential areas into segregated quarters.

Six main questions are dealt with in this chapter.

1. What was the role of religion—specifically Islam—in the development of the form and spatial patterns of Iranian cities?
2. What are the urban requirements of Islam, and how were Iranian cities transformed into Islamic cities after the seventh century A.D.?
3. What is the role of the mosque in a traditional Iranian city, and what other institutions are associated with it?
4. What are the main imprints of Shiʿite Islam on the Iranian townscape?
5. What features of a traditional Iranian city are related to the role of the government and to the social structure of the city's population?
6. How, and why, are residential areas divided into segregated neighborhoods?

Religion and the City

Religious belief in Iran (as elsewhere) has been an influential factor affecting all aspects of citizens' lives, including their sociopolitical organization and the form of their cities. Early organized religions were introduced with the arrival of the Aryans (around 1700 B.C.) in the Iranian Plateau; they merged with, and replaced, the former religions practiced by the natives of the plateau.[1]

Around 600 B.C., Zoroaster introduced Zoroastrianism to the Iranian people, a religion that worshiped Ahura Mazda (the God of Light), who was in constant battle with Ahriman (the God of Darkness). The basic message of salvation by the prophet Zoroaster was attained by three major acts of faith: good deeds (*kirdār-i nīk*), good (pure) thoughts (*pandār-i nīk*), and good words (*guftār-i nīk*).[2]

*Ātashkadih*s or fire temples were the most important religious centers of pre-Islamic Iranian cities (the larger *ātashkadih*s were known as *ātashgāh*s). They were places of worship, as well as the main cultural centers where the holy fire was kept burning. Located at the center of the city, they were readily accessible to the majority of the Zoroastrian population. In addition to their religious functions, the *ātashkadih*s served as the locus for social gatherings and economic, educational, and political activities (Zaehner 1961). After the arrival of Islam in Iran in the seventh century A.D., these buildings were gradually replaced by the congregational (community) mosques. Mosques took over the religious and cultural duties of *ātashkadih*s and became the main religious centers of Iranian cities.

Not too long after its introduction, Islam became the main religion practiced by the Iranian population. Since its arrival, Islam has not only affected the spiritual life of the Iranian population, but to a great degree has also influenced the form and structure of settlements: Islamic religious buildings form some of the most significant structures even in contemporary Iranian cities.

In traditional Iranian cities, as well as in modern ones, the main religious buildings are the mosques, *madrasih*s (*madrasa*s or religious schools), *imāmzādih*s (shrines of Shiʿite *Imām* descendants), *ḥusaynīyyih*s (buildings for religious mourning), and *mazār*s and *pīr*s (culturally respected shrines). These religious structures are examined below.

The Mosque

The mosque was introduced to Iranian cities by Arab Muslims in the seventh century. Being the main place of communal worship and prayer, the mosque soon became the symbol of a Muslim city. During the first few centuries of Islam, a settlement without a major mosque was not considered a city (Gibb and Kramers 1953; Grabar 1969).

After the fall of an Iranian city to the Muslim invaders, the city went through structural changes to meet the needs of the new Islamic state. As an example, the Zoroastrian *ātashkadih*s were often replaced by mosques. This addition of the mosque was the major physical change brought to Iranian cities by Islam. In many cases (for instance, in the city of Sāvih), the great Zoroastrian fire temple was made into a prominent mosque. This was accomplished simply by the addition of some major elements of the mosque, such as the *miḥrāb*, the *minbar*, and later on the *minārih* to the old structure.[3] (The structural elements of the Iranian mosque are discussed in appendix C.) In some other cases, the Arab conquerors destroyed the fire temples, rather than convert them into mosques. This was frequently the case when the population resisted or when the Arab leaders simply chose this course of action. In these cases, new mosques were erected on or near the sites of the former fire temples.

Mosques were located where they could be reached by Muslim city dwellers, as were the former fire temples. The Masjid-i Jāmiᶜ or main community mosque (also called the Congregational Mosque) is built in the form of a large, tall building, often at the center of the city, either along the main bazar or very close to it. Since the most important weekly community prayer is performed on Friday in this main mosque, the Masjid-i Jāmiᶜ is also called the Masjid-i Jumᶜih (Friday Mosque), a more familiar term to Western scholars. As the tallest building in the city, the Masjid-i Jāmiᶜ is visible from different parts of the city, mainly through its tall minarets. It is within easy walking distance of the majority of the population, and particularly of the *bāzārī*s.

In traditional Iranian cities, the Masjid-i Jāmiᶜ becomes the focal point of the bazar. Arthur Pope (1967: 3/909) explains this:

> Hence the Friday mosque particularly is veritably the home of all the people. Such a complex institution, serving so many purposes, religious, political, social, and educational, must of necessity correspond in plan to the multiplicity of functions. As it is spiritually coextensive with the whole life of the city, so it becomes physically integrated with the texture of the city. Therefore it is rarely set apart, but in most cases, as we read with wearisome iteration in the Arab geographers, is close by the city market or bazaar, and nearly always the congregational mosque is continuous with the densely crowded structures of the town. It is emphatically marked by the great portal and dome, but there is no cathedral close, or even a parvis. In most cases one cannot walk around the mosque. Besides the portal it has no facade and often no discoverable outer walls. It is, perhaps, the only impor-

> tant architectural structure in the world the area of which is undefined. It literally melts and merges into the surrounding buildings.

There has been great emphasis on the importance of the Friday Mosque and its centrality within traditional Islamic cities (Von Grunebaum 1955; Planhol 1959; Pope 1967) to such a degree that the other elements of the city have been nearly ignored. For instance, Pope (1967: 3/909) writes: ". . . the mosque is the city, or rather the focus of the city, and its physical ambiguity represents a definite spiritual fact and purpose. It records the city's life and growth and comprises many secular and all its spiritual functions."

There is no doubt that the mosque is a mandatory element of the Iranian Muslim city; in some cities like Iṣfahān, mosques such as Masjid-i Jāmiᶜ actually record many centuries of the city's life and growth. However, Pope seems to exaggerate the importance of the mosque—particularly where Iranian cities are concerned—at the expense of other major elements of the city such as the bazar and even similar religious elements like the *imāmzādih* and *ḥusaynīyyih*. Very often in traditional Iranian cities, the latter elements are more important to the city than the Friday Mosque, as shown later in this chapter.

In a traditional Iranian city, the Friday Mosque is often considered one of the main elements of the bazar complex and, in many cases, the focus of the bazar, where there are more crowds and activities. However, unlike the popular belief postulated by the model of the Islamic city, it is not the mosque but the bazar that forms the center and actual focus of the typical traditional Iranian city.

The Masjid-i Jāmiᶜ, customarily the main mosque of the city,[4] is often located along the bazar at the intersection of two major *rāstih-bāzār*s. It is the focal point of the entire bazar complex, accessible to the majority of the *bāzārī*s, as well as to the rest of the population.

Certain economic activities are centered around the mosque, to fulfill its needs. The religious rituals practiced in the mosque and the educational classes held there (as well as in the *madrasih*s) require special equipment supplied by the nearby shops. Therefore, shops selling goods such as *muhr*s (small tablets made of clay from sacred cities), *tasbīḥ*s (rosaries), perfume, candles, books, papers, and pencils are found in *rāstih-bāzār*s around the mosques.

Another reason for the mosque's location close to the bazar is its frequent use by the *bāzārī*s. According to Islamic religious requirements, adult Muslims must perform their prayers five times a day; in addition, there is a hadith (prophetic saying) that indicates that prayers said in a mosque are twenty-five times more effective than those said elsewhere (Gibb and Kramers 1953). Therefore, it is much more convenient for the *bāzārīs* to have their mosques located within a few minutes' walking distance from their shops.

The role of the mosque in traditional Iranian cities has been compared to that of the cathedral in the medieval European cities (Pope 1967). It is primarily the place of worship, where the entire Muslim population of the city can participate in the congregational prayers. Here, between the times of prayers, the religious leaders hold their teaching sessions either in sanctuaries or in the courtyard. These religious leaders are also available to the common people of the community who come to them for religious counsel. However, as Pope has noticed, compared to the cathedral, the mosque is a more social institution; it puts less emphasis on religious rituals and is more open to secular activities (Pope 1967).

The mosque is often used as a resting and washing place for tired travelers and is also the home for many poor and homeless people at night. It is a meeting place for friends and strangers who exchange religious information, as well as political and commercial news. It also functions as a place where the rulers and commoners can come in contact with each other. In old times, royal decrees, notices of taxes and tax exemptions, and other news items concerning citizens' affairs were posted in mosques.[5]

The mosque's role in the sociopolitical history of Iran is very prominent. The gathering of huge crowds in large mosques and the potential for mass demonstrations, especially after emotional speeches by popular religious leaders during Shiʿite holy days, make the mosques very effective in the unification of the people in demanding certain political changes. The role played by the mosque in the 1979 Revolution, which resulted in the fall of the monarchy and the establishment of the present Islamic Republic of Iran, testifies to this situation. During the time of unrest between 1977 and 1979, mosques in different Iranian cities were places of opposition to the shah's regime. Antiregime speeches by religious and community leaders were delivered at the mosques. *Bāzārīs*, who usually are more regular mosque goers, closed their shops and participated in increasing mass demonstrations against the regime. The closures of the bazars, as in Tehran, were followed by the closures of other major economic enterprises (such as oil production centers), which resulted in the eventual collapse of the shah's government.

Due to its multifunctional quality, the mosque, from the beginning, became a main public center in the city. Like the bazar, it is a major gathering place. The basic difference between the Friday

Mosque and the bazar is the fact that—unlike the bazar, which is the communal place for people of different religions, ethnicity, and socioeconomic backgrounds—the Friday Mosque is only accessible to the Muslim population. This feature of the Friday Mosque—plus its smaller size compared to the bazar—makes it the second major gathering place for the people of traditional Iranian cities. The exceptions to this are cities with major holy places and *imāmzādih*s, such as Mashhad and Qum, whose holy shrines are the most crowded centers of the city at all times.

Mosques are also educational institutions; religious teaching sessions are held in the larger and more popular mosques. There are always *mullā*s (Islamic religious teachers) residing in the mosques to teach youngsters the Qurʾān (Koran) and basic reading and writing of the Persian language. Adults receive their education in *madrasih*s, usually attached to the great mosques or very close to them within the bazar complex. In addition, mosques usually have their own libraries, which in many cases include secular as well as religious collections.[6]

The importance of the mosque to Iranian Muslim cities—and especially to the bazar—is so great that people of certain trades and professions often build their own mosques. There is a hadith of the Prophet Muḥammad that says: "For him who builds a mosque, God will build a house in Paradise" (Gibb and Kramers 1953: 335). The building of mosques is also a sign of social prestige and an indicator of the material wealth and religious piety of the builders. The mosques built by people of particular trades, such as shoemakers, carpetsellers, clothsellers, and blacksmiths, can still be seen in the major Iranian bazars. These mosques are usually located along the same *rāstih-bāzār*s as the shops that are occupied by their builders; for instance, a clothsellers' mosque is located along the clothsellers' *rāstih-bāzār*.

Mosques are also built by people of similar origin, who usually live in the same neighborhood. Many mosques are also built in residential areas. Political and community leaders display their degree of religiosity by building mosques. However, the great mosques, including many Friday Mosques, are those that have been built by the royal families of different dynasties that ruled the country.[7]

Mosques are not concentrated only along the bazars; they are also scattered around the city, within the residential areas, so that each neighborhood has at least one mosque. Neighborhood mosques are located at the center of each residential district (the *maḥallih*), along the local bazar and next to a few other public structures. The adult population of the *maḥallih*s regularly meets in the local mosque to discuss problems related to the area, such as security, water, garbage disposal, and loitering youth. Social and family affairs such as marriages, divorces, mourning, celebrations, and so on are also discussed in local mosque sessions (*maḥallih*s are examined in more detail later in this chapter).

Shiʿite Urban Requirements and Iranian Cities

Shiʿite Muslims share with Sunni Muslims (who form the majority of the world's Muslim population) the belief in Muḥammad and the holy Qurʾān. They also share basic religious requirements, such as regular daily prayer (*namāz* or *ṣalāt*), daytime fasting (*rūzih* or *ṣawm*) in the month of Ramażān or Ramadan, pilgrimage to Mecca (*haj* or *hajj*), almsgiving (*zakāt*), and profession of faith (*shahādat* or *shahāda*). However, they differ with Sunni Muslims over the recognition of the true successors to the spiritual leadership of Islam or caliphate (*khalāfat*). According to Sunnis, the *khalāfat* after Muḥammad the Prophet goes to Abū-Bakr, ʿUmar, ʿUthmān, and ʿAlī, in turn.

Shiʿites in Iran believe that the *khalāfat* after the prophet continues through the line of ʿAlī (the Prophet's cousin and son-in-law) in the series of the Twelve *Imām*s. The Twelfth *Imām,* Mahdī (Lord of Time, Ṣāḥib-i Zamān), will return as the savior, bringing justice when the world approaches its end (a religious concept also held by Zoroastrianism, the pre-Islamic religion of Iran).[8] These *Imām*s—most of whom were murdered by their enemies—are worshiped by the Iranian Shiʿites as martyrs of Islam; their shrines, as centers of pilgrimage, are sacred and highly respected. Although Iran currently has the largest Shiʿite population, it contains only the shrine of Imām Rižā in Mashhad; the rest are buried in the present countries of Iraq and Syria. However, Iran contains numerous shrines of saints who are believed to be descendants of the Shiʿite *Imām*s. These shrines are known as *imāmzādih*s.

The martyrdom of the third Shiʿite *Imām,* Ḥusayn (Hussein), in Karbalā, stands as the most important event in the history of Shiʿism as practiced in Iran. Husayn's tragedy in Karbalā has influenced many aspects of Iranian culture, including city buildings. The events in Karbalā are commemorated in the buildings constructed for this particular purpose. These buildings are known as *ḥusaynīyyih*s (or *ḥusaynīyya*s), named after Ḥusayn himself.[9]

While mosques are common features in all Islamic cities, *imāmzādih*s and *ḥusaynīyyih*s are usually peculiar to the Shiʿite sect of Islam. They are not commonly found in the cities inhabited by

Sunni populations. Due to their functional importance in Iranian cities, *Imāmzādih*s and *ḥusaynīyyih*s are discussed below.

*Imāmzādih*s. *Imāmzādih* literally means a descendant of an Imām. An *Imām* (*emam*) in this case is a person whose roots can be traced to one of the Twelve Shiʿite Muslim *Imām*s. In practice, however, the word *imāmzādih* refers to the shrine or the building in which a descendant of an *Imām* is buried. These holy shrines are scattered throughout the country, and most of them are thought to be the Imām Riżā's (the Eighth Shiʿite Muslim *Imām*) brothers, sisters, cousins, or other close relatives.

*Imāmzādih*s, when located within cities, form one of the major core areas. In Iran, the religious importance of these buildings often surpasses that of the Friday Mosque. They often become the major visiting and gathering places of citizens, as well as pilgrims. Figure 30 illustrates a major gathering in front of the Imāmzādih Yaḥyā in Sabzivār, during a religious commemoration. Figure 31 shows a religious procession proceeding toward the same *imāmzādih*. The *imāmzādih* usually contains a dome-shaped structure, in which the saint is buried; the dome is decorated by a layer of tilework and is usually accompanied by one or two decorated minarets. *Imāmzādih*s also include sanctuaries for communal prayers and other religious rituals. A courtyard with fountains, pools, and gardens usually serves visitors and pilgrims both for sacred ablution and for aesthetic purposes. *Imāmzādih*s receive their visitors from the city, the hinterland, or neighboring cities. Many *imāmzādih*s are attached to one or more *kārvānsarāy*s, which are used as lodging places for pilgrims.

Many of these *imāmzādih*s do not have reliable historical records to authenticate the identity of the person buried there. Some of these are even assumed to be graves of old Zoroastrian holy men, whose followers declared them to be Muslim saints. This was done to prevent the destruction of their tombs by fanatic Muslim religious leaders (Spooner 1963).

*Imāmzādih*s were so important in Iran that in many cases they were the main reasons for the initial establishment or future development of cities. A prime example of this is the great city of Mashhad, the second largest city of modern Iran.

Mashhad was a village named Sanābād at the beginning of the ninth century A.D. During that century, Imām Riżā, the Eighth Shiʿite Muslim *Imām*, was poisoned (according to Shiʿite belief) and buried in this village. The celebrated shrine of Imām Riżā attracted visitors and pilgrims from different parts of the Shiʿite world; the

Figure 30. Sabzivār: Imāmzādih Yaḥyā; the crowd has gathered to commemorate Muḥarram at the main center of the city.

Figure 31. Sabzivār: a religious procession on its way to Imāmzādih Yaḥyā for a passion play.

small village of Sanābād developed into a major city. The name was changed to Mashhad—place of martyrdom of Imām Riżā—and gradually became more important than its two contemporaries, the ancient cities of Nīshābūr (Nīshāpūr) and Ṭūs. These cities were located in Khurāsān, a province in northeastern Iran. Ṭūs was destroyed during the first decades of the thirteenth century by Mongols, and the surviving population moved to the town of Mashhad. Mashhad thus replaced Ṭūs and became the main city of the Khurāsān district.

The area surrounding the shrine (called *ḥaram* or the holy quarter) contains courts, mosques, sanctuaries, *madrasih*s, *kārvānsarāy*s, and bazars; it still forms a town by itself. Until the middle of the twentieth century, a wall around the area separated the holy quarter completely from the rest of Mashhad. As the main center of the city, the *ḥaram* was a hub from which many streets and alleys radiated outward. The streets were hemmed by the city wall, which was rebuilt many times as the city grew during different historical periods (Sykes 1910).[10]

Due to its extraordinary religio-cultural importance, the *ḥaram* (the main *imāmzādih*) has always been the main urban core of Mashhad. Its location has influenced the structure of the city in such a way that the morphology of traditional Mashhad does not follow that of most other Iranian cities. Most cities developed mainly as trade centers with the bazar as their central core. In Mashhad, on the other hand, the *ḥaram* forms the true center of the city.

The traditional city of Mashhad was circular and fit into the model of the Islamic city developed by scholars such as Von Grunebaum (1955). The holy quarter (*ḥaram*) formed its heart and the bazars that roughly radiated from this central structure formed the commercial zones. The residential zones encircling the commercial district were connected to the central zone by way of several roads usually intersecting in the *ḥaram* area. Houses had access to these roads by way of numerous narrow winding streets (Fraser 1825; Sykes 1910). Figure 32 shows the compact city of Mashhad, centering on the holy quarter; the holy quarter itself is seen in figure 33; the new twentieth-century roads have been superimposed on the old ones.

The spatial pattern and segregation of trade within the bazar also conform to that of the Islamic city model. The main difference between Mashhad and this model is that, instead of the Friday Mosque, an *imāmzādih* (the shrine of Imām Riżā) forms the center of the city. Considering the functional similarity of shrines and mosques in Iran, Mashhad fits well into the model of the Islamic city.[11]

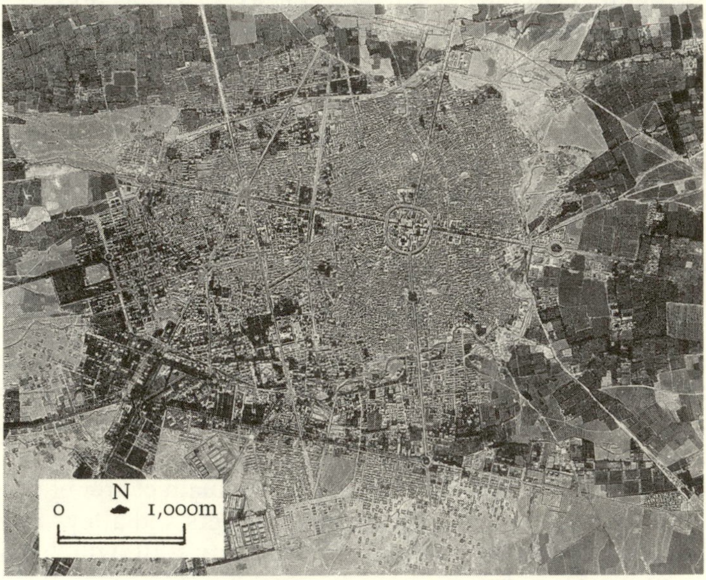

Figure 32. Traditional city of Mashhad developed around the shrine of Imām Riżā (1956 aerial photograph, National Cartographic Center, Iran; original scale 1 : 40,000).

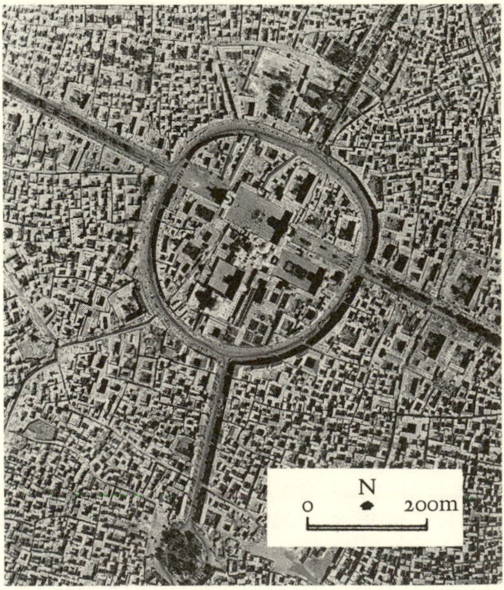

Figure 33. The *ḥarām* in Mashhad (1956 aerial photograph, National Cartographic Center, Iran; original scale 1 : 6,000).

Although religious elements are the main factors that accelerated the growth and development of Mashhad, other factors contributing to its growth should not be ignored. For example, in addition to becoming a major religious center, Mashhad was located along the roads that connected northern Iran to central Asia (Bukhara, Samarqand, Khwarazm, and on to China), Afghanistan, and the southeast (via Sīstān), to the Hīrmand (Helmand) Basin. It was, therefore, a suitable place for caravans to rest and trade their merchandise. Relatively good climatic and agricultural conditions also facilitated this growth.

Mashhad is located 3,000 feet above sea level in the fertile valley of the Kishaf-Rūd (Kishaf River), which runs from the northwest to the southeast of the country. Its high altitude and proximity to the mountains give Mashhad a pleasant climate, quite amenable to human habitation. In addition to the Kishaf-Rūd, various qanats irrigate Mashhad, and the city is famous today for its surrounding orchards and the production of canned fruits.

Being located along various trade routes, having a fertile hinterland, and enjoying a favorable climate were also major factors contributing to the development of Mashhad as a major city. However, the main reason for its continuous growth was (and remains) the popular shrine of Imām Rizā located at its core. Mashhad is known as the city of Imām Rizā; it is highly respected and holy in the eyes of Iranian Shiʿites. Many kings and political leaders have paid particular attention to improving this city.

The morphology of Mashhad (like many other Iranian cities) is also an example of the political leaders' impact on the planning and configuration of Iranian cities. Many kings, for religious purposes as well as for propaganda and self-aggrandizement, personally contributed to the development of the city by building great mosques, *madrasih*s, bazars, and other facilities. Shah ʿAbbās I (reigned 1587–1629), the great king of the Safavids, for example, traveled on foot from his capital, Iṣfahān, to Mashhad, to show his respect for the shrine of Imām Rizā. After reaching the city, he ordered improvements in the structure and decoration of the shrine and built many *kārvānsarāy*s and other public facilities. During the reign of Nādir Shāh (1736–1747), Mashhad became the capital of the country and experienced its most flourishing times. Many of the city's structures date from this period (Ṣani ʿal-Daula 1885).

*Imāmzādih*s are scattered throughout the country. They vary in their importance and in their degree of centrality within the city, according to their family heritage and closeness to the Twelve Shiʿite

*Imām*s. Not all of the shrines are *imāmzādih*s; some of them are tombs of saints or religious teachers.[12]

Frequently, the burial place of a famous poet or of a social, cultural, or political leader becomes very important to Iranian cities, serving as a gathering place and tourist attraction. The tombs of Hāfiz and Saʿdī in Shīrāz; Ibn-i Sīnā (Avicenna) and Bābā Tāhir in Hamadān; Firdausī in Ṭūs; and Nādir Shāh in Mashhad are some examples of this. These shrines are known as *mazār*s (*ārāmgāh*s, *maqbarih*s). The shrine of Muslim Sufi saints known as *pīr*s are found inside and outside the cities and receive many pilgrims from neighboring areas. The second most important Shiʿite structures of Iranian cities after *imāzādih*s are *ḥusaynīyyih*s.

*Ḥusaynīyyih*s. *Ḥusaynīyyih*s are religious buildings built in memory of Imām Ḥusayn (Hussein), the Third Shiʿite *Imām*. As previously mentioned, according to Shiʿite belief, Ḥusayn—along with a group of his followers—was martyred (680 A.D.) in a war against the army of Yazīd, the caliph of the time (Sykes 1910; Momen 1985). In these buildings, people gather and mourn the death of Ḥusayn and his relatives.

*Ḥusayniyyīh*s consist of a large courtyard usually surrounded by rooms. During the month of Muḥarram—the month in which Ḥusayn was killed—these buildings are filled with faithful mourners. All day, and part of the night, one can hear *mullā*s (religious teachers) or *rauẓih-khān*s (preachers) describing the tragedy of Karbalā (the city in present Iraq where Ḥusayn was attacked by the army of Yazīd). Frequently, the courtyard of the *ḥusaynīyyih* is used for the passion plays that depict this story. The major *ḥusaynīyyih*s are usually located along the main bazars at the core of the city, and the smaller ones are scattered in different neighborhoods.[13]

Building *ḥusaynīyyih*s—like building mosques—is an indication of religious piety, social prestige, and professional unity. This is particularly true among the professionals in the bazar complex. In Sabzivār, for example, one can see the Ḥusaynīyyih-yi ʿAṭṭār-hā (Grocers' Ḥusaynīyyih), Ḥusaynīyyih-yi Bazzāz-hā (Clothmakers' Ḥusaynīyyih), Ḥusaynīyyih-yi Qannād-hā (Candysellers' Ḥusaynīyyih), and so forth. Like mosques, *ḥusaynīyyih*s are also scattered throughout the city: each residential neighborhood has its own. The courtyard of a *ḥusaynīyyih* is usually covered by canvas during the month of Muḥarram, when it is most used (this is particularly true when Muḥarram is in the rainy season). If the neighborhood does not have a *husaynīyyih*, then the local mosque is used for the same purpose during Muḥarram.

During Muḥarram, people of similar profession or of the same neighborhood organize into groups and prepare a religious procession. During the day, the procession leaves the local *ḥusaynīyyih*, where it has been prepared, and moves throughout the city stopping in major religious centers such as *imāmzādih*s, the Friday Mosque, and other major *ḥusaynīyyih*s. A procession (*hayʾat* or *dastih*) is formed by a group (or several groups) of mourners who are dressed in black shirts with openings in the back or chest area. While moving along the major streets within the city, they walk behind another group carrying black or green flags with religious slogans written on them (green is the color of the turban of those whose roots go all the way to Banī Hāshim, the clan to which Muḥammad the Prophet and the Twelve Shiʿite *Imām*s belonged). In many processions, the men dress as different characters and represent the tragedy of Karbalā. During the procession the men in black shirts stop periodically and beat their naked chests with their palms or hit their backs with chains (see fig. 31). While doing this, they chant with the actor-leaders who read poetic lamentations relating to the death of Ḥusayn and his followers.

The tragedy hits its peak when the procession approaches the core of the city. When it stops in an *imāmzādih, ḥusaynīyyih,* or mosque, for example, the *sīnih-zanān*s (those who beat their chests) and *zanjīr-zanān*s (those who hit their backs) put on their best performance. At this point the actors dramatize the tragedy of Karbalā, eliciting lamentation and tears from the audience. After finishing the circuit through the city, the procession goes back to the starting point, where there is a feast prepared for the members of the procession. After the feast, the mourning ceremony continues until late into the night.

The direction of the movement of the procession within the city and the stopping points, besides emphasizing the important religious centers, display the existing social hierarchy. The procession also stops at the residence of the large landowners, important religious leaders, and some other influential inhabitants of the city. The map of movement of a procession within the city of Sabzivār, as shown in figure 34, demonstrates the spatial representation of religious and social hierarchy within the city.

Sociopolitical Structures and the City

Thus far, the public structures of the traditional city, such as the bazar and its associated religious structures, have been discussed. In the remainder of this chapter some other public elements of the city

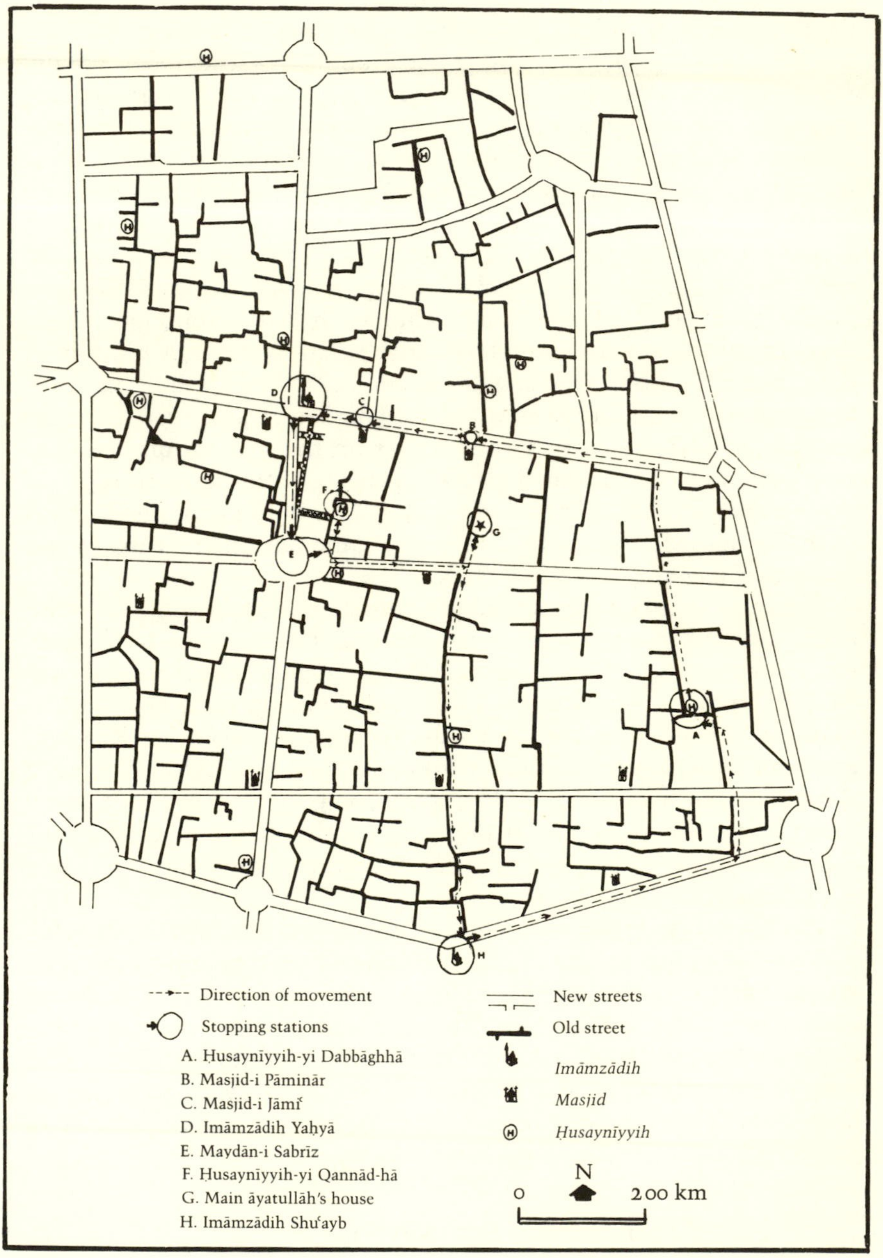

Figure 34. Movement of a Muḥarram procession within the city of Sabzivār.

are examined in relation to the sociopolitical structure. Finally, the residential neighborhoods and their configuration within the city are discussed.

The sociopolitical structure of Iran has its roots long before the emergence of Islam. It has been built around absolute monarchs, who were claimed to have derived their powers from God and who were supported by important religious leaders.[14] In addition to clerical alliances, they were supported by powerful landowners, military personnel, and important merchants, who also formed the most influential classes of Iranian society.[15] Artisans, craftsmen, laborers, and farmers formed the lower classes. In traditional Iranian cities, community leaders were chosen from the members of influential classes to govern the administrative affairs of the city.

Traditional Iranian cities did not possess municipal governments, as was common in preindustrial European cities (Sjoberg 1960; Falamaki 1977). Most of the services were provided by the neighborhood or community leaders, and each city quarter was responsible for its own well-being. The activities of community leaders were controlled by the *dārūghih* (chief of police) and the *kalāntar* (the king's appointee), who acted as the city governor (Arasteh 1964: 21).

Usually the *arg* (palace) was the seat of the government, where most of the political and military activities took place. Depending upon the size and status of the city in different historical periods, the form and function of the *arg* varied. Under some powerful leaders, in large cities that served as capitals and had a particular strategic or political importance, the *arg* was considered the most significant urban element, forming the largest and most centralized structure of the city. For example, in Shīrāz, which served as the capital of the Zand Dynasty (1750–1794), the *arg* was the seat of Karīm Khān, the founder of the dynasty. In cities with significant strategic importance the *arg* also served as the citadel, where the rulers' armies practiced their regular exercises. Two examples of these are Qalʿih-yi Falak al-aflāk in Khurram-ābād, and Qalʿih-yi Shūsh in Shūsh (*qalʿih* means citadel in Persian).

*Arg*s were built in an easily defensible place, usually on high terrain, where control of the city and its gates was possible. In smaller cities, it was one of the main elements, often in direct relation with the Friday Mosque and the bazar. In many cities the bazar connected the Friday Mosque and the *arg,* acting as a bridge between religion and politics (or in a common Iranian expression: Dīn va Daulat). Often the frontage of the *arg* was the *maydān,* another major element of the traditional city.

The city contains at least one major *maydān,* a large public square located either near the gates or at the center of the city. Smaller *maydān*s form the centers of residential neighborhoods. In many cities a large *maydān* is the entrance to a major bazar. Examples are Maydān-i Naqsh-i Jahān in Iṣfahān, Maydān-i Ganj-Alī-khān in Kirmān, and Sabzih Maydān in Tehran. They are particularly used as gathering places during major religious, political, or sociocultural events: rituals related to the two holy months of Muḥarram and Ramażān, political events such as elections and executions, and the celebration of Persian holidays, especially Naurūz (the spring equinox—the beginning of the Persian New Year).[16] On ordinary days, *maydān*s are occupied by retailers who sell their products in booths.

Browsing in the bazars, participating in religious and cultural events, performing the rituals that take place in the religious buildings and *maydān*s, and visiting friends and relatives are the major recreational activities of the traditional Iranian population. However, some other places such as a *zūr-khānih* (literally meaning house of strength), *qahvih-khānih* (coffeehouse), and *bāgh* (park) are also used for recreation.[17]

*Zūr-khānih*s are traditional Iranian gymnasiums, originating in pre-Islamic times (Arasteh 1961; Bahar 1976). They are places for body-building and the establishment of fraternities for the improvement of moral virtues, peculiar to Iranian culture and not found in other Muslim cities. Admission to the *zūr-khānih* requires a good social, as well as religious, reputation as a selected member of the community.

The traditional *zūr-khānih* is a dome-shaped structure usually located along the bazar, where it is easily accessible to its users. The main section of the *zūr-khānih* is the *gaud,* a hexagonal or octagonal field with a resilient clay floor about one meter below ground level. It is located beneath the dome with an area of some ten to thirty square meters, providing room for the athletes to exercise, wrestle, and so forth. Four areas are above ground level around the *gaud:* the most elevated is for the athletic leader (the *murshid*), with his drums and gong; the second space is the dressing area for athletes; the third area is for spectators; and the remaining area is for storage of equipment.[18]

Another important social gathering place in the traditional city is the *ḥammām* or public bathhouse. *Ḥammām*s are health and social institutions where people go to bathe, massage, shave, and converse, found in all traditional cities of the Islamic world. They are important elements of Iranian cities and are distributed evenly within them. Usually there is a *ḥammām* near each major mosque, for the purpose of sacred ablution prior to prayers. However, contrary to some scholars' opinions, they are not considered attachments to mosques (see Von Grunebaum 1955; Planhol 1959). *Ḥammām*s are also found in places where there is neither a mosque nor any other religious building. Each residential neighborhood has its own *ḥammām*.[19]

*Ḥammām*s are built of stone or fired brick (they are too damp for the dried mud-brick that forms most of the other buildings). To conserve heat, *ḥammām*s are usually built into the ground with the vault, dome roofs, chimney, and an entrance above ground. The water, usually provided by a qanat, flows by gravity down through the heating chamber (burning brush and wood fuel) and into the baths. The smoke runs into ducts under the bath floor to heat the rooms above before exiting through the chimney. The *ḥammām* has at least two rooms: a changing room, where people sit on raised slabs in niches around the walls, facing each other; and a large bath hall, with similar raised seating slabs around the walls, a communal hot pool, and a warm pool to rinse in. People soak in the hot bath; on the raised slabs they rub themselves (or one another), usually with a rough piece of cloth (*kīsih*) that has been treated with soap, and rinse themselves with water drawn from the rinsing pool. Usually there are workers (*dallāk*s) who do the cleaning and rinsing. The larger *ḥammām*s have a more complicated plan with many different rooms. From the entrance to the hot bath, the rooms become progressively hotter. People often spend hours in a *ḥammām*, a comfortable place for relaxing and socializing.

While the bazar and its associated elements (*masjid*s, *madrasih*s, *imāmzādih*s, *mazār*s, *ḥusaynīyyih*s, *maydān*s, *zūr-khānih*s, *ḥammām*s, etc.) form the focus of public life, private life takes place in residential areas within segregated neighborhoods or *maḥallih*s.

Residential Areas: The Maḥallih System

In traditional Iranian cities, residential areas are segregated into different *maḥallih*s. People of similar interests or backgrounds cluster together in their own *maḥallih*s for comfort, protection, and greater security. The division of *maḥallih*s is based on differences in ethnic background, religion, profession, or town or village of origin. Thus, a *maḥallih* is a spatial residential cluster of members of a particular ethnic group within the city.

Examples of the segregation of *maḥallih*s based on differences of religious beliefs can be seen in the Jewish *maḥallih* (*juhūd maḥallih* or *maḥallih-yi yahūdi-hā*) in Iṣfahān and the Zoroastrian *maḥallih* (*gabr maḥallih*) of Kirmān and Yazd. Other examples are Arab, Turk, or Armenian *maḥallih*s.

Segregation according to religion or ethnicity is mainly seen in the larger Iranian cities, with larger, more diverse populations. In smaller towns, due to cultural homogeneity, the basis for the division of *maḥallih*s is the difference in profession or origin. For example, in city of Sabzivār, with the exception of the gypsy *maḥallih* (*maḥallih-yi kaulī-hā*), there is no *maḥallih* based on ethnicity or religion.

In Sabzivār *maḥallih*s are based on differences in profession and place of origin. This is indicated by the names: *maḥallih-yi zargar-hā* (goldsmiths' *maḥallih*), *maḥallih-yi āhangar-hā* (ironsmiths' *maḥallih*); *maḥallih-yi turk-ābād* (the *maḥallih* of those from the village of Turk-ābād), *maḥallih-yi Daulat-ābād* (the *maḥallih* of those from the village of Daulat-ābād). *Maḥallih*s are also named after their main cultural feature or geographical landmarks. Some examples from Sabzivār are *maḥallih-yi arg* (citadel *maḥallih*), *maḥallih-yi ḥammām-i ḥakīm* (Ḥakīm bathhouse *maḥallih*), and *maḥallih-yi sar-dih* (head village *maḥallih*). Sometimes the *maḥallih* is named after one of the influential leaders residing there. For example, again in Sabzivār, one can see the *maḥallih-yi Āqā* (the *maḥallih* where Āqā, a religious leader, used to live).

People of the *maḥallih* select members to administer the affairs of the *maḥallih*. They create laws and rules to regulate social relationships. Although these laws are known and obeyed by residents, there are no documents indicating the fact that these laws have ever been officially written (Falamaki 1977, 1978). Today, in traditional sections of Iranian cities, the practice of these oral laws can still be observed. For example, the children and female population of the *maḥallih* are protected by the young men, who have the duty of providing the *maḥallih* with police protection. If a female member of the *maḥallih* is offended by an outsider, it is the duty of the young men to find the offender and punish him. Sometimes these young men become overzealous, and a small incident turns into an angry feud that strains the relationship between the two *maḥallih*s for a long time. Disputes between *maḥallih*s may also be caused by traditional rivalries, past incidents or grievances, and water rights.

An interesting aspect of the development of *maḥallih*s in traditional Iranian cities was the lack of social class segregation. The rich did not cluster in exclusive groups away from the poor. In many cases the rich and poor lived in the same neighborhood, sometimes next door to each other. There were many reasons for this. First, and probably foremost, was the family structure that obligated the more fortunate to support the less fortunate in the family. This prevented any embarrassment that might arise from the poverty and deprivation of a close relative.[20]

Islam encourages this kind of coexistence between the rich and the poor; its teaching about the worthlessness of this mortal materialistic life, and the high value of the immortal spiritual life, is a concept that pious Muslims keep constantly in their thoughts. Traditionally, it is the duty of every financially well-to-do Muslim to live with the less fortunate and to see that no neighbor suffers from hunger or malnutrition.

Although differences in ethnicity and origin were the main reason for the initial formation of the *maḥallih*s, the system also helped the overall organization of the city. In addition to gathering people of similar ethnic background together, the division of cities into *maḥallih*s served as a system for administration, control, taxation, and other city affairs, such as better water management.

The residential district, as the main private zone of the city, has a completely different way of functioning than the crowded bazar. Nevertheless, they have an organic relationship with one another. By providing the bazar's main market, the residential district is a complement to it. From the smallest unit within the city (the private house), to the cluster of residential units (the *maḥallih*), to the main city center (the bazar), all are strongly interrelated and have cell-like connections. The households obtain their services from both the *maḥallih* center and the bazar. The everyday needs of the residents are supplied by the *maḥallih,* and more esoteric and expensive goods are supplied by the central bazar. The *maḥallih* centers are in constant contact with the bazar and neighborhood shops and receive their supplies through the bazar merchants. In short, the *maḥallih* is well integrated into the city.

The majority of space in each *maḥallih* is devoted to private residences along narrow pathways. The focus of the *maḥallih* is a central square, usually located at the intersection of two or more primary streets. This central square is called *markaz-i maḥallih* (*maḥallih* center). Around the central square are a group of shops and a few public buildings. The shops usually cater to the everyday needs of the residents, including a butcher, bakery, grocery, and fruit sellers. The number and variety of shops depend on the size and importance of the *maḥallih* within the city.

Some larger *maḥallih*s in more important cities have their own *bāzārchih* (small community bazar) with shops that also provide their local customers with some other goods such as clothing, shoes, and furniture. One may also find local craftsmen there, such as a tailor or a carpenter, who have their workshops within the *bāzārchih*, along the main *guzar*, or somewhere around the square. A main *guzar* or *rāstih* connects the *markaz-i maḥallih* to the main city bazar, where the residents can shop for other than everyday needs.

The public buildings located in the center of the *maḥallih* provide the residents with water and with religious, social, and recreational services. Each *maḥallih* center usually has a mosque and a bathhouse to provide the local population with a center for prayer and a place for the sacred ablution required prior to praying. Other buildings in the *maḥallih* center may include the *ḥusaynīyyih, zūr-khānih, āb-anbār* (water cistern), *qahvih-khānih* (coffeehouse), *mazār* (shrine of a saint) or *imāmzādih*, and *madrasih*. In some *maḥallih*s, the *ḥusaynīyyih* serves as a local mosque, used for prayers as well as religious rituals. Not all of these buildings necessarily exist in a single *maḥallih*, particularly the smaller ones, though larger *maḥallih*s usually include them all. In the arid regions of Iran, a water cistern is one of the main required public buildings, and at least one is always found in any *maḥallih* center. Usually there are several water cisterns in each *maḥallih*, located along the main alleys and serving different neighborhoods with cold, fresh water.

All *maḥallih* centers serve the residents around them, and all are connected to the bazar by primary streets or *guzar*s. Tavassoli (1982) describes one of the main *guzar*s in Yazd, known as *guzar-i yuzdaran*, which passes through two of the main *maḥallih*s: Khūshk-i Nau and Fahāddān. The two centers of these *maḥallih*s are located at the intersection of *guzar-i yuzdaran* and two other primary streets. The center of Fahāddān *maḥallih* includes a *bāzārchih, maydānchih* (small *maydān*), *zūr-khānih, āb-anbār* (water storage), *ḥusaynīyyih, masjid, madrasih*, laundry (a postindustrial phenomenon), and *mazār* or holy shrine (Tavassoli 1982).

In the center of the Khūshk-i Nau *maḥallih*, one can still see a *ḥusaynīyyih*, a mosque, a water cistern, a *bāzārchih*, and a dyer's workshop. There are also remnants of an old gate to the *maḥallih*, a water mill, and an abandoned *kārvānsarāy* (Tavassoli, 1982).

The width of the access roads has an indirect relationship to the degree of privacy. The narrowest access routes or *bunbast*s are used exclusively by the residents of houses along them or by their visitors. They are the common property of the local residents. *Kūchih*s, though not considered private property, are not exactly public either; they are usually used only by the residents of the *maḥallih*.

Although the central square is the focus of the *maḥallih*, social activities continue along the *kūchih*s too. For example, women from neighboring houses gather together and sit on a platform in front of their *hashtī*. While socializing, they do part of their daily work such as weaving, sewing, or knitting. The small alleys, particularly the *bunbast*s, are used by the residents of the *maḥallih* and for all practical purposes belong to them. This gives a sense of privacy: a stranger (a nonresident of the *maḥallih*) cannot help but be scrutinized while in the neighborhood.

The primary streets (*guzar*s) are wider *kūchih*s and have greater use. They connect the neighboring *maḥallih* centers to one another and also to the bazar. They are usually used by the residents of those particular *maḥallih*s to gain access to the bazar. The bazar, or the main center of the city, is the only place that can be used by anyone, under any circumstances.

Summary

Islam, and particularly its Shiʿite branch, has had a significant impact on the development of the form of traditional Iranian cities. After the arrival of Islam in the seventh century, the mosque replaced the *ātashkadih* as the main religious center of the city. The main city mosque (the Friday Mosque) is usually the focal point of the bazar complex.

The imprint of the Shiʿite sect of Islam is seen in traditional Iranian cities in the form of *imāmzādih*s, *ḥusaynīyyih*s, and *mazār*s. These buildings, like mosques, function as the main religious, cultural, and political centers of the city. In some cases (as in Mashhad) their religious importance surpasses that of the Friday Mosque and they serve as the city's main gathering places. The sociopolitical structure of Iranian society traditionally has also required city structures such as *maydān*s, *zūr-khānih*s, and *arg*s.

These buildings are all associated with the bazar, both spatially and functionally. Most public activities of the city occur within the bazar and related structures. These structures are unique physical entities and are spatially distinguished from one another. However, functionally, there is considerable interrelationship among the types of activities occurring within them. For example, the mosque and the *ḥusaynīyyih* often function in a similar manner, and the *maydān* is also used for religious purposes as much as for political or commercial purposes. This can be related to the role of Islam in Iran, a religion that is not only a spiritual faith, but a way of life for its adherents.

Private life is centered in segregated residential neighborhoods or *maḥallih*s, divided according to differences in ethnicity, religion, profession, and/or place of origin. However, differences in profession and place of origin, rather than ethnicity and religion, are the bases for *maḥallih*s in smaller cities and towns.

CHAPTER FIVE

SUMMARY AND CONCLUSIONS

THE MAJOR INTENTION throughout this study has been to show what factors have been responsible for the formation and development of Iranian cities. Many factors have been historically involved with the formation and development of Iranian cities, the most important of which (such as the physical environment, trade and historical events, religion, and sociopolitical structures) have been discussed in detail.

The physical geography of the Iranian Plateau, ancient trade routes, and religious and political decisions are the main factors determining the selection of sites for Iranian cities. However, physical environment is clearly the most significant factor. It also influences the location and direction of the major trade routes. The main ancient trade routes followed the central desert fringe, parallel to the bases of the Alburz and Zagros mountain chains. Access to water and an arable hinterland were also primary conditions for the survival of a city.

Generally speaking, the cities that have survived throughout Iranian history are those that were built at the foothills of mountain chains or in intermountain basins; were located along (or close to) the ancient trade routes; had access to water (mainly through qanats); and had relatively arable hinterlands. It is important to note that this also includes the cities that had their origins in religious and political decisions. Cities such as Sulṭānīyyih (built away from the major trade routes in an area without adequate water and arable hinterland) did not survive after the death of their founders. Unlike cities built on suitable sites, they failed to grow organically.

The interrelationship of factors is more evident where the internal structure of traditional Iranian cities is concerned. For example, the compact city, with its homogenous buildings, served a variety of purposes. It was appropriate for the climatic conditions of the Iranian Plateau, conserving more land for agricultural uses. The compact city also facilitated social cohesiveness and provided a convenient traffic system. This form also offered close proximity of different land uses as well as easier defense and, last but not least, responded to requirements of Islamic-Iranian culture (such as the need for communal worship, seclusion of women, privacy, etc.). Thus, the morphology of traditional Iranian cities was the product of multiple factors that are closely interrelated.

How intricately are these factors related to one another? While the majority of Iranian cities evolved out of agricultural settlements, trade played a major role in their development. The bazar became the core of the city and influenced the pattern of urban growth. Although it developed as a commercial center, the bazar became the center for cultural, religious, and political concerns as well. This factor in particular distinguishes traditional Iranian cities from the so-called traditional Islamic city with the Friday Mosque at its center. City structures related to public activities were located along, or very close to, the bazar. Although these structures were spatially distinguished from one another, they were closely integrated functionally. For example, mosques, *ḥusaynīyyih*s, and *imāmzādih*s were used for religious as well as social, cultural, and political purposes and the *maydān* housed commercial as well as religious, social, and political activities.

The high degree of religious influence in Islamic societies (such as that of Iran) has promoted some scholars to consider the Middle Eastern townscape a vivid reflection of Islam. Although the Islamic influence in Iranian urban form should not be underestimated, its influence should not be exaggerated either. It has been demonstrated that Islam in general, and Shiʿite Islam in particular, left its imprint on Iranian townscapes by the establishment of buildings such as mosques, *imāmzādih*s, and *ḥusaynīyyih*s. However, it has been shown that other elements such as the physical environment, trade, and political history have played equally significant roles in the morphology of Iranian cities.

The spatial pattern of the city (including the location of the bazar, the Friday Mosque, the *arg*, *maydān*s, *ḥammām*s, *zūr-khānih*s, *maḥallih*s, etc.) was as much a response to religion as it was to the economy, Iranian sociocultural structure, or historical incidents (e.g., the decision of a king to build a bazar, a mosque, or other structures near his residence). The form and pattern of the city were also a response to environmental factors such as heat, wind, and dust. In the discussion of residential units, for example, it has been shown that the form of a traditional Iranian house is as much a reflection of Islamic requirements as of the climatic conditions of the Iranian Plateau. It has also been pointed out that the development and organization of *maḥallih*s within the city were affected by ethnic and religious patterns as well as other factors, such as place of origin of the inhabitants.

Thus, it must be said that these factors are so closely interrelated that the mention of one without the others is inadequate in speaking of the Iranian city. While each factor is significant, no single element can be held individually responsible for the formation and development of the spatial patterns and morphologies of cities in Iran.

The formation and development of the physical form of traditional Iranian cities is a synthesis of many different factors that emerged over several thousand years of city life in the region. It is impossible to identify one single factor as the main definer of the morphology of the traditional Iranian city, be it Islam, trade, or the physical environment. However, what makes the traditional Iranian city unique, and a valuable source of study for future urban planners, is its responsiveness to the Islamic-Iranian culture and the great harmony between its structural design and the natural environment of the Iranian Plateau.

Another major inquiry of this study has been whether there is a rationale behind the physical form of traditional Iranian cities. Throughout this study we have seen how several interrelated factors have influenced the development of spatial patterns and morphology of traditional Iranian cities and how these factors relate to the location, form, and function of various physical elements of the city. For example, the strong desire for privacy and tranquillity divided the city into two major parts: the bazar area (the center for public activities) and the residential zone (the place for private life). Differences in ethnicity, religion, profession, and place of origin led to the development of *maḥallih*s (segregated residential neighborhoods).

Examination of the environmental aspects of traditional urban forms has demonstrated how effectively the general structure of the traditional city (compactness, lack of open space, uniform buildings, street form and orientation, and housing structure) reduced the effects of the hostile climate, such as intense solar radiation and strong, harmful, dusty winds. At the same time, the traditional city utilized available natural forces to provide means of comfort.

Thus, traditional Iranian cities are not simply a "tangle of blocks badly ventilated by a labyrinth of twisted alleys and dark courts"

(Planhol 1959: 1). On the contrary, they have been planned to satisfy the cultural needs of their users and, at the same time, to deal with the pragmatic realities of heat, dust, and shortages of water.

There is a distinct order to the form of traditional Iranian cities. They were patterned on a human scale. As seen in the discussion of street patterns, when the topography permitted, streets in most cities followed a geometric pattern (grid and/or radial). A hierarchy of street size and function formed the traffic network of the traditional city. The circulation system consisting of different-sized pathways and the bazar was not random, but quite rational in its design.

Today most traditional cities have been disrupted by the imposition of new urban developments. The old bazar and residential quarters have been built over and often replaced by new wide avenues and apartment complexes. Elements of the old town are often destroyed and replaced by new structures without any consideration of their cultural and ecological importance. Known as "old towns," traditional cities now languish adjacent to the new cities. They are mainly inhabited by the urban poor, who often cannot afford to repair their dwellings.

The new city is the twentieth-century outgrowth of the old town, often surrounding and spreading out from the traditional city nucleus. It contrasts sharply with the old town; the new city is sprawling and diffused, stretching over a large area, with wide avenues arranged primarily in grid patterns and Western-style houses and apartment complexes. It is an imitation of modern Western cities, not necessarily suitable to the hostile arid climate of the Iranian Plateau and incompatible with local cultural needs.

There are many lessons to be learned from a close observation of traditional Iranian cities. The morphology of these cities has evolved over the past few millennia. The inhabitants of the Iranian Plateau gradually learned through this long period how to deal with the hostile physical environment of the region. They effectively employed their limited resources and adopted an architecture that enabled them to build their cities in such a way that they could cope with their environment. They harnessed the possible natural forces and, by reducing the undesirable climatic stresses, created better living conditions.

Studies such as this one that assess the value of traditional urban planning may help future Iranian (as well as other Middle Eastern) urban planners to reevaluate their contemporary city-growth policies. Although many aspects of modernization are valuable to Iran and other Middle Eastern countries, modern urban forms and technological innovations need to be blended with local physical and cultural needs, not merely adopted with total disregard for the local conditions. Instead of imitating the modern cities designed by Western planners, whose environments and cultures are vastly different from those of the Middle East, Middle Eastern planners may be persuaded to employ the indigenous experiences of the past, to bring back a sense of continuity, and a link to the present. Not all that relates to the past need be demolished.

APPENDIX A

QANATS AND SETTLEMENTS IN IRAN

MOST IRANIAN SETTLEMENTS are found within the large alluvial fans in the pediment zone between the mountains and deserts, including cities such as Tehran, Iṣfahān, and Kirmān. A majority of settlements receive an annual precipitation (between 100 and 300 millimeters) below the minimal requirement for crop production and do not possess major rivers with enough discharge for agricultural seasons. How have they survived through the ages and created one of the oldest civilizations? The answer lies in the availability of subsurface water that has been diverted and brought to the settlements by the genius of primitive technology through the subterranean aqueduct known as the qanat (or *kārīz*) in Iran.[1]

The *qanāt* is a subterranean aqueduct that collects groundwater at the foot of the mountains and carries it by gravity through a gently sloping tunnel, cut into alluvial material, to the fields and settlements (see fig. 6).

Construction of Qanats

Traditionally, qanats have been constructed with hand labor by a group of skilled men, called *muqannī*s (or *kārīz-kan*s) in Iran, who often transfer their craft to their heirs. The traditional tools used by *muqannī*s were a hatchet, a short-handed shovel, a small oil lamp, and the windlass located at the mouth of the shaft, on the surface. The first step in construction of a qanat is finding the location of the first shaft or mother well (in Persian *mādar-chāh* or *chāh-i mādar*). The *muqannī* usually follows the track of the main gullies coming from the hills and looks for evidence of water such as a spring, seepage, vegetation like long-rooted summer plants, or some other clues that help him to estimate the approximate location of the mother well.[2] This mother well is dug until it reaches the groundwater of an impermeable stratum. The well is approximately one meter in diameter and as deep as the water table of the area. The depth of the mother well also depends on the length of the qanat, the size and gradient of the alluvial fan, and the amount of the owner's investment.

Within each basin in the Iranian Plateau there is a decrease in the depth of the mother well from the foot of the mountains toward the central desert. The deepest wells are located close to the foothills, where the water table is deep beneath the surface and the water is sweet. The shallowest wells are close to the edge of the desert, where the water table is close to the surface and water is salty. In the cities of Sabzivār and Shāhrūd, where the alluvial fans are small with more gradient, the majority of qanats have a depth of some fifty meters. The large and less steep alluvial fans of Tehran and Qazvīn allow a depth between ten and twenty meters (Beaumont 1971). The deepest mother well has been reported as a 275-meter qanat near Bīrjand (Noel 1944). Due to the expense of construction, qanats are kept as shallow as possible; they are seldom dug below 100 meters.

To find out where the water will flow out onto the surface, the fall in the ground between the mother well and the outlet of the qanat (in Persian *maẓhar-i qanāt*) is calculated. To minimize the degree of erosion of the tunnel by running water, the gradient should be somewhere between 1 : 1,000 and 1 : 1,500 or a nearly horizontal tunnel. It is not always possible to have the mouths of the qanats in the settlements. English (1966a) mentions that the qanats of Māhān and Jūpār (south of Kirmān) cannot be completely submerged because their mother wells are located about two to three thousand feet higher than these settlements in the foothills of the Jūpār Mountains. In these cases, the qanats must flow on the surface for many miles before reaching the settlements, which increases the dangers of pollution and evaporation during the hot seasons.

The length of the qanat is the distance from the mother well to the outlet. Like the depth, it depends on the slope of the ground and the depth and slope of the water table. Within any basin, qanats are short in the steeply alluvial deposits at the foot of the mountains and become longer as they approach the less steep surfaces toward the desert. Around Yazd and Kirmān in the margin of the desert, qanats are as long as fifty kilometers (English 1968); in the alluvial deposits of the foothills of Shāhrūd and Sabzivār, they are less than five kilometers in length (Beaumont 1971). The longest qanat reported is approximately seventy kilometers, near Kirmān (Noel 1944). However, most qanats in Iran are less than five kilometers long.

When the location of the mother well and outlet and the direction and gradient of the qanat have been determined, the tunnel is constructed. Usually, construction of the qanat begins from the outlet in an upslope direction toward the mother well. But when time is a factor, two *muqannīs* start the construction from two sides and dig toward each other. In intervals of 50 to 100 meters a series of vertical shafts (*chāhs*) are dug along the qanats to connect the tunnel to the surface. The function of these shafts is to ventilate the air and remove the excess dirt during construction and to provide access to the tunnel if repairs are necessary. The excess dirt is collected around the mouths of the shafts and is used to protect the shafts against shifting sands and flooding.

The tunnel is dug in an egg shape or an elliptical cross section about 1 meter wide and 1 to 1.5 meters deep. When the tunnel passes through sandy soils, baked clay loops are used to prevent roof and wall collapse. The tunnel continues to be dug in an upslope direction until the water from the water table seeps in.

In the construction of a qanat, there is always danger of drowning under rushing water, being buried by collapsing roofs, suffocation, sliding while climbing up and down the shafts, snakebites, and so forth. Therefore, the *muqannīs* are usually well paid and respected among the villagers. The construction of qanats always starts with some religious ceremony and many ritual preparations.

The amount of discharge determines the value of qanats. It depends on production capacity of the aquifer and the length of the water-bearing section, which in itself is related to the amount of precipitation. The discharge of a qanat varies during the year with fluctuation in the height of the water table. Some qanats in Iṣfahān and Shāhrūd have a discharge of about 900 cubic meters per hour, but most qanats have a discharge between 0 and 80 cubic meters per hour (Beaumont 1974). The maximum discharge occurs in winter and early spring and the minimum discharge in late summer and fall. Comparing discharge patterns and climatic data, Beaumont illustrates a definite correlation between precipitation and discharge in the city of Mashhad (Beaumont 1971).

Qanats and Village Settlement Patterns

Due to their expense and importance, qanats have played a major role in the social structure and settlement patterns of Iranian villages. They often pass under the owners' summer rooms and emerge somewhere on their properties. After passing through the village and satisfying domestic needs, qanats are used for agricultural purposes.

The more prosperous people live around the outlet or upstream (in Persian *bālā-āb*) where the water is fresh and clean, and the peasants live downstream (in Persian *pāyīn-āb*) where the water is already warmed and polluted. However, the householders usually obtain their drinking water early in the morning when the water is still fresh and clean. The hierarchy is the same for agricultural lands (Beckett 1951).

Qanats and Deep Wells

Of some 40,000 qanat systems in Iran today, less than 25,000 remain in operation, and this number will tend to decrease with time. They are being replaced by deep wells, introduced to Iran by the Allied Armies during World War II. The number of deep wells had increased from a handful to 7,400 by 1970 (Beaumont 1974). The main advantage of wells over qanats, in the farmers' view, is cheaper construction costs. As has been pointed out, the construction of qanats is very expensive and time consuming. English (1968) mentions that the construction of a 3-kilometer qanat near Kirmān, with a group of laborers working every day, took seventeen years to finish, at a construction cost of about $10,000 per kilometer. Comparing these figures with those required for a deep well (one to two months for construction and $3,000–15,000) compels an economy-minded farmer to choose the well over the qanat. Although qanats do not require extra expenses for operation after construction, their water supply is not controllable and is wasted during nonagricultural seasons. Even in agricultural seasons, without construction of a reservoir in the direction of the outlet, the water is unused during the night.

Qanats, however, unlike the pumped wells, are in balance with nature and their discharge is regulated by the groundwater table, while wells control the groundwater and can be abused. In the plain of Varāmīn, Beaumont (1968) indicates that the water table has fallen in parts of the region as a result of the use of pumped wells, leading to a significant reduction in use and in some cases to abandonment of many qanats that irrigate the plain. (Similar problems were seen in several rural areas in the vicinity of Sabzivār during 1984–1985).

Although their number has decreased, qanats still represent the best response to the problem of water shortage and the physical setting of the Iranian Plateau. In many regions of the plateau around the deserts, where the water table is shallow, stagnant, and mineralized, wells are not workable and qanats remain the only alternative.

APPENDIX B

STRUCTURAL ELEMENTS OF THE BAZAR

THE TRADITIONAL Iranian bazar was the center of public life; the main public activities of the city dwellers and visitors occurred in and around the bazar.[1] To satisfy the public's needs, the bazar contained a number of structures with architectural designs and locations suitable for hosting different public activities; they were also easily accessible. The activities within the bazar had economic as well as noneconomic roots. A classification and description of these activities with respect to their spatial arrangement within the bazar follows.

I. ECONOMIC ACTIVITIES
   A. Trade
   B. Storage and Warehousing
   C. Production
II. NONECONOMIC ACTIVITIES
   A. Religious
   B. Educational
   C. Sociopolitical
   D. Recreational
   E. Services

This classification is made only for the convenience of this study. In a traditional society like that of Iran, in which religious, political, economic, and other activities are closely interrelated, separation of the structural elements of the bazar by their particular function always involves the risk of oversimplification. Nonetheless, only elements related to economic activities are studied below. The elements in the bazar listed under noneconomic activities are presented in chapters 3 and 4.

Economic Activities

Elements Related to Trade Activities

The main elements involved in trade activities within the bazar are the *rāstih-bāzār, chahār sū, tīmchih,* and *khwān.* However, trade is often practiced in tandem with production and other activities, as is the case in the *qayṣarīyyih* and *sarāy,* described in the section on elements related to production.

Rāstih-bāzār. *Rāstih-bāzār*s are the long stretches of the bazar lined with shops and other commercial buildings on both sides. They are the meeting places of customers and shopkeepers, the most crowded and noisy areas of the bazar complex. Each bazar complex contains several major *rāstih-bāzār*s, which themselves give way to minor *rāstih-bāzār*s, and other elements such as *sarāy*s and *dālān*s. Figure 35 illustrates a typical Iranian bazar, with its economic elements.

Chahār sū. *Chahār sū* literally means four-sided, referring to the space created when two main *rāstih-bāzār*s intersect. They have been also called *chahār sūq*s, meaning the place where four bazars meet (*sūq* means bazar in Arabic). *Chahār sū*s are often decorated with a central fountain pool that provides pleasant, moist air, particularly welcome during hot summer days. They are covered by domes, higher than the domes of the neighboring *rāstih-bāzār*s and often decorated with glass and tilework. *Chahār-sū*s serve as the main meeting places of *bāzārī*s and other users of the bazar. The largest *chahār sū* in the bazar (the *chahār sū buzurg*) was used as the administrative center of the bazar and also served as the headquarters for the *dārūghih,* the chief of police (Najmi 1983).

Tīmchih. A *tīmchih* is the major meeting place for merchants, where most business contacts are made. The rooms of the *tīmchih* are mainly used as offices of the bazar merchants, with few storage or production activities conducted there. These main centers of business activity are usually located within the bazar, between a *rāstih-bāzār* on one side, and a *sarāy* or *kārvānsarāy* on the other (see fig. 35).

*Tīmchih*s are two or three-story buildings, usually round or hexagonal in shape, with rooms surrounding a small central pool. Their ceilings are often decorated with glass, plaster, and/or tilework and are quite elegant architecturally. Each *tīmchih* is devoted to a par-

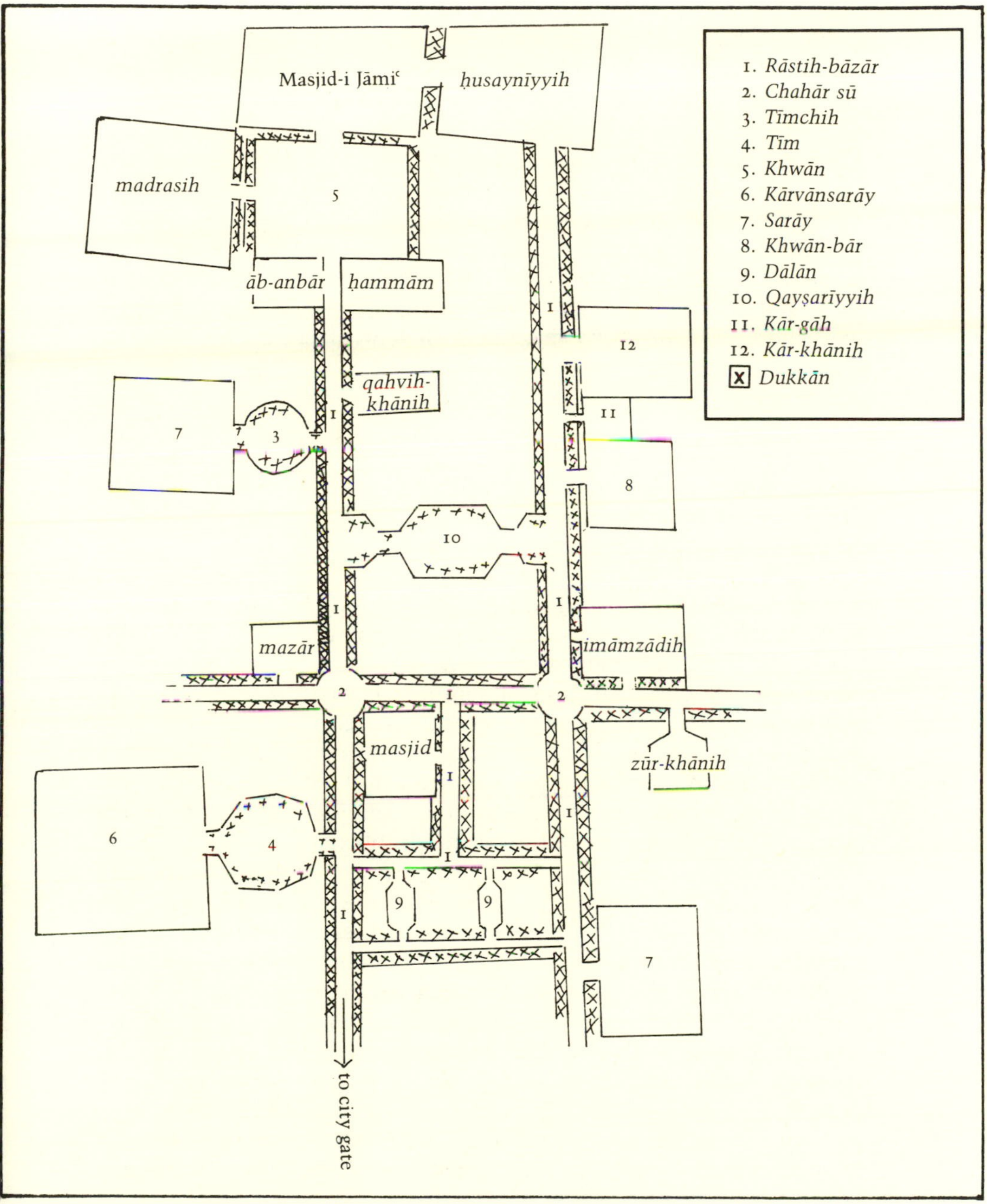

Figure 35. Elements of a typical Iranian bazar.

ticular trade and often owned by a single merchant, whose name is given to the building (for example, Tīmchih-i Ḥājī Ḥasan: Ḥājī Ḥasan's Tīmchih). The larger *tīmchih*s are often referred to as *tīm*s; due to their larger size, they are devoted to more than one trade.

Khwān. *Khwān*s are large *maydān*s (squares) that contain entrances to major *rāstih-bāzār*s on one or more sides. They are usually surrounded by one or more public buildings such as mosques, *madrasih*s, *ḥusaynīyyih*s, *imāmzādih*s, *āb-anbār*s (cisterns), or *ḥammām*s. However, there are always some empty spaces next to these public buildings that are reserved for use as retail shops or workshops. *Khwān*s also serve as gathering places during political and cultural events.

Elements Related to Storage Activities

Of the group of buildings used primarily for the storage of goods prior to their circulation within the bazar, the *kārvānsarāy, sarāy,* and *khwān-bār* are the most important.

Kārvānsarāy. *Kārvānsarāy*s, literally meaning houses of the caravans, dotted the countryside, either within the cities or outside them along the old trade routes. Those within the cities were located near the entrance gates and along the main *rāstih-bāzār*s. In addition to their role as major economic centers, they were also major cultural centers, serving as the gathering place of merchants and travelers from different parts of the world. At least as old as the bazar itself, *kārvānsarāy*s remain, continuing to serve as the major storage and trade centers of the bazar complex.[2]

*Kārvānsarāy*s located outside the cities were almost always situated along the commercial routes where there was an adequate supply of food and water. This supply was necessary because cities in Iran were (and still are) located quite far from one another—caravans could not travel the distance between neighboring cities without stopping for food and rest. In addition, *kārvānī*s also did a significant amount of trade with the rural population that had settled around these buildings. *Kārvānsarāy*s outside the cities were well fortified, providing protection for their users against any raiding nomads, brigands, or natural hazards such as the sand-laden storms that are common in central Iran. They functioned as protected forts, water and food stations, resting places, storage areas, and trade centers.

There was at least one *kārvānsarāy* in each cluster of major *masjid*s, *madrasih*s, *imāmzādih*s, or *mazār*s. Pope (1967) asserts that *kārvānsarāy*s served mainly pilgrims and other users of these holy places and may have even owed their site selection to religious rather than economic factors. Since most *kārvānsarāy*s were not necessarily located near religious structures and their main function was trade and lodging, Pope's hypothesis does not seem to be true.

*Kārvānsarāy*s, whether inside or outside cities, were generally built in a rectangular shape. At the center there was a pool, often decorated with one or more fountains and surrounding gardens, with the water provided by qanats or wells. This pool was the center of a rectangular, unroofed courtyard, which was itself surrounded by a roofed, rectangular, usually two-story structure containing rooms on both the first and second floors. Rooms on the first floor were used for storage, and those on the second floor as guest rooms. Larger rooms (often in the center of each side or in each corner) were used by wealthy merchants or other distinguished guests. The entire complex was surrounded by a wall, set one or two meters from the buildings. The space created between the wall and the main structure was roofed and used for housing animals. This area was kept cold and dark to minimize the proliferation of flies and other insects (Pope 1967). The surrounding wall contained a guard tower on each corner, and two larger guard towers were usually built above the entrance gates to the building itself.

*Kārvānsarāy*s inside bazars were located along *rāstih-bāzār*s or between branches of the bazar. Their basic design and structure were similar to those located outside the cities, but they were not usually as spacious. Fortification was less important for bazar *kārvānsarāy*s; they were used more for economic purposes than for any other use. Their main function was to store goods for wholesaling and distribution among the shops within the bazar. Very often access to the *kārvānsarāy* was gained through a short, narrow hallway that connected the *rāstih-bāzār* to the courtyard of the *kārvānsarāy*. This hallway, acting as a *bāzārchih* (small stretch of bazar), contained a large wooden door at the courtyard end that was locked during the night when the bazar was closed. Both sides of this hallway were lined with shops and stalls that served as merchants' offices and often were used to display the newly arrived merchandise stored in the adjoining *kārvānsarāy*.

Sarāy. *Sarāy*s were much like *kārvānsarāy*s, only smaller. As the name might indicate, *sarāy*s, unlike *kārvānsarāy*s, did not provide lodging for *kārvānī*s (caravan members); they were primarily used only for the storage of merchandise and contained offices where trading activities were conducted. *Sarāy*s were always built as part of

Figure 36. Sarāy-i Ḥāj-Zamān, an active *sarāy* in Sabzivār, is still functioning as an economic center.

Figure 37. A working *sarāy* in the traditional city of Sabzivār.

the bazar and, unlike *kārvānsarāy*s, could not exist independently (outside of a bazar) since trading activities were the sole reason for their existence. Although different, *sarāy*s are often not distinguished from *kārvānsarāy*s due to their physical resemblance. Many Iranian-made maps showing Iranian bazars lump *sarāy*s and *kārvānsarāy*s together, calling them all *sarāy*s. This may be due to the fact that the present usage of the old *kārvānsarāy*s no longer includes housing *kārvānī*s.

*Kārvānsarāy*s and *sarāy*s still form the major centers of trade throughout bazars (see fig. 36 and 37). However, *kārvānsarāy*s that are located outside cities are no longer maintained for economic purposes. The *kārvānsarāy*s located along the old, isolated trade routes have been abandoned, and those along newer roads are used mainly by the army for mobile divisions.

Khwān-bār. Also known as *anbār-i kala*, *khwān-bār*s were warehouses and did not contain any commercial offices or guest rooms. Their rooms were larger than those of the *sarāy*s, giving them the capacity to store more goods. They were often situated close to workshops that dealt with the division and packaging of goods into standardized amounts.

Elements Related to Production Activities

Production activities usually took place in the bazar in two different forms: in the *kār-khānih* (factories) that were independent of retail selling and in shops and smaller workshops whose business did include retail selling. Production activities within the bazar complex were mainly conducted in the *dālān* or *band*, *qayṣarīyyih*, *kār-gāh*, and *dukkān*.

Dālān. A *dālān* or *band* was a corridorlike structure that connected two *rāstih-bāzār*s. A *dālān*'s architecture and physical appearance were similar to a *rāstih-bāzār*'s, but shorter and narrower. It was also lined with workshops on both sides that sometimes reached as high as two stories. Because it was closed off from the noise of the two *rāstih-bāzār*s by doors at either end, the *dālān* provided a peaceful working place for craftsmen and artisans. Depending on its location within the bazar, it could be occupied entirely by tailors or quilters or other professionals. The *dālān* was generally occupied by people of the same profession or closely related professions, such as spinning and carpetmaking.

Qayṣarīyyih. A *qayṣarīyyih* was also a hallwaylike structure that connected two *rāstih-bāzār*s, but was wider than a *dālān*. Like the *dālān*, it contained a door at each end that opened to each *rāstih-bāzār*, which was locked during the night. *Qayṣarīyyih*s were often the sites of the production and retail sale of expensive goods such as jewelry or silk products. Usually built and owned by wealthy *bāzārī*s, *qayṣarīyyih*s were quite elegant in design and architecture. Most were decorated with detailed plaster sculpture and tilework and formed the most architecturally attractive nonreligious buildings within the bazar complex. Like *dālān*s, they were built up to two or more stories. The upper stories usually contained the retailers' workshops, while the rooms on the first floor, easily accessible to customers, were used for retail selling.

Kār-gāh. *Kār-gāh*s were workshops, places for industrial production, as in *kār-gāh-i najjārī* (carpentry workshop). Smaller *kār-gāh*s were usually accompanied by a retail shop. They were located along the *rāstih-bāzār*s, and craftsmen of similar trades had their *kār-gāh*s next to one another in the same *rāstih-bāzār*.

Kār-khānih. *Kār-khānih*s (meaning houses of work) were factories or places for industrial production and work assembly. They consisted of several spacious buildings connected to one another; each building's design and architecture varied from its neighbors', depending on the type of operation involved. *Kār-khānih*s were located within the bazar next to *kārvānsarāy*s or at the outer margin of the bazar complex between the commercial and residential zones. Some *kār-khānih*s, such as tanneries, were located outside the bazar at the edge of the city because of negative factors associated with their operation. Tanneries, for example, emitted unpleasant odors. The most common type of *kār-khānih* within the bazar complex was the *kār-khānih-yi pārchih-bāfī* (textile factory).

Dukkān. *Dukkān*s (literally meaning shops) were the smallest units within the bazar; functioning as retail shops, they lined both sides of the *rāstih-bāzār*. Neighboring *dukkān*s usually dealt with similar trades; for example, one *rāstih-bāzār* was assigned to shoe-selling *dukkān*s, another to carpet-selling *dukkān*s, and so on. Many *dukkān*s also contained a small workshop in the rear for the production of finished goods. The larger *dukkān*s could be divided into as many as three sections. The front was the retail area where the shopkeeper also kept his desk and papers. The second section was the *kār-gāh* or workshop, which was either directly behind the retail area or, in the case of two-story buildings, directly above the shop. The third section was for storage—usually a small space attached to the workshop. In *dukkān*s, the workshop and storage areas were hidden from the eyes of customers, but the retail portion was decorated to attract passersby.

APPENDIX C

STRUCTURAL ELEMENTS OF THE MOSQUE

ARCHITECTURALLY SPEAKING, mosques were built in rectangular shapes, with an internal courtyard surrounded by the area of sanctuary. The sanctuary (known as *shabistān*) to the south of the mosque was larger and was considered the main *shabistān* of the mosque. Sanctuaries were divided into different sections by columns, usually made of brick.[1] The floors of the sanctuaries were covered by carpets or *qilīm*s (less expensive cotton carpets roughly woven compared to delicate Persian carpets). Spaces between columns were used by *mullā*s (religious teachers) who leaned back against these columns and received those who came to them for religious counsel. The *mullā*s also held their classes here between the hours of prayers. On sunny days the courtyard was used for communal prayers and class sessions. It was usually packed with people during the holy months of Muḥarram and Ramażān.

The main elements characterizing a mosque are the *minārih* or minaret (called *guldastih* in the eastern provinces of Iran), *miḥrāb*, *minbar*, and *vużū-khānih* (place of sacred ablution).

In order to be visible from different parts of the city, mosques—particularly larger ones—had minarets standing tall at the corners of the buildings overlooking the surrounding city structures. These minarets usually formed the tallest structures in traditional Iranian cities (church spires served the same function in traditional European cities). In addition to its function of visibility, a minaret contained a roomlike structure at its top that was used by the *muʾazzin* (who called people to prayer at different times of the day). In Iran these minarets usually were (and continue to be) decorated with colorful tiles and represented some of the best architectural works of the mosques. Minarets face the *kaʿba* (*kaʿbih*). The location of the *kaʿba* (the cubic house of God in Mecca, Saudi Arabia) is significant in Islam. It forms the central focus of the entire Muslim world and is the point to which all Muslims must face while conducting their prayers. This direction toward the *kaʿba* is called *qiblih* (or *qibla*). The *miḥrāb* is a nichelike structure carved in the wall indicating the *qiblih* in each mosque. Each *shabistān* (prayer hall) usually has its own *miḥrāb,* which can be compared to the altar wall that is seen in many Christian churches, adorned with the image of Christ or a saint.[2] The *pishnamāz* (leader of communal prayers) stands against the *miḥrāb* with his face toward it, while the devotees line up behind him in rows, facing the same direction. With a series of harmonic movements, the devotees follow the *pishnamāz*'s lead, listening to the guiding voice of the *mukabbir* (usually a boy who announces the proper times for rising, bending, and prostrating, for the people in the back rows who cannot see the *pishnamāz*'s movements). The *miḥrāb* is usually decorated with tiles and glass, forming the most sacred part of the mosque.

Due to Iran's geographical location in relation to Mecca in Saudi Arabia, *miḥrāb*s in Iranian mosques always face southwest. The orientation is so vital that sometimes the whole building must be specially oriented in order for prayer halls to face the *qiblih.* Frequently this orientation is not in harmony with the preexisting street pattern or morphology of the square on which it stands. A good example of this is the Shah's Mosque (Masjid-i Shāh, built during the seventeenth century A.D.) in Iṣfahān, located on the southern side of the famous Shah's Square. In order to face the *qiblih,* the mosque has been skewed several degrees in such a way that its orientation no longer follows that of the square (which had been built with the same orientation as preexisting structures of the city, such as the older square left from previous dynasties).[3] This pattern exists throughout the Muslim world.[4]

Another part of the mosque is the *minbar,* a steplike structure, always located against the *qiblih* wall to the right of the *miḥrāb.* Built of wood or brick, it is used as a seat for the preacher before and after the communal prayers. *Minbar*s are located in prayer halls and are also found in the courtyard, located against the *qiblih* wall.

Some mosques also contain a pool with a fountain in the middle of the courtyard for the ritual sacred ablutions before prayer, as well as for recreational purposes. However, due to the need for more space in the courtyard at the time of public gatherings, most mosques do not contain this feature. In place of the pool there is usually a building connected or very close to the mosque to fulfill the purpose of religious cleansing. This building is called the house of sacred ablution (*vuẓū-khānih*) and in bigger mosques includes several pools ornamented by fountains, gardens, restrooms, and one or more water storage rooms (*āb-anbār*s). The ablution pools and restrooms used by women are segregated from those used by men. Some of these buildings also include one or more halls for prayer.

NOTES

1. Introduction

1. For early accounts of Islamic cities, see Sauvaget (1934); Pauty (1951); Von Grunebaum (1955: 141–158); and Planhol (1959).

2. For example, see Von Grunebaum (1955: 141–158).

3. See Hourani and Stern (1970: 9–24). See also Abu-Lughod (1987).

4. Master plans, known as *ṭarḥ-i jāmiʿ*, are development plans for various cities produced by the Ministry of Housing and Urban Development, Architectural and City Planning Unit. They are put together by a group of professionals in a variety of disciplines (e.g., urban planners, architects, civil engineers, geographers, historians, economists, sociologists, etc.) so that each master plan includes information on the historical, geographical, and other characteristics of the city.

5. The two other major Iranian cartographic centers consulted were the Saḥāb and the Gītā Shināsī (both in Tehran), whose materials were used during this study.

2. The Physical Environment and the City

1. According to some scholars, the term "Iranian Plateau" refers to the upland from eastern Anatolia and the Caucasus in the west to the plains of the Punjab in the east. For more information, see Fisher (1968).

2. For more information about qanats, see English (1968); Wulff (1968); Beaumont (1971); and Goblot (1979). A good study of qanats can also be found in the new edition of the *Encyclopaedia of Islam* (1975) under "Kanat."

3. For a good study of architecture and urban planning in arid regions, see Fathi (1986). See also Olgyay (1963) and Golany (1978, 1983).

4. The term *kūchih,* in traditional cities, was a common expression referring to any pathway (except the bazar) within the city.

5. This model is based on the author's considerable personal observation of streets in traditional parts of various Iranian cities and descriptions of traditional cities by designers of master plans.

6. *Hashtī* literally means octagonal. In practice, however, it referred to any covered polygonal space located immediately behind the entrance door to the house.

7. For example, see Planhol (1959: 1).

8. Information for this section was obtained through fieldwork, interviews with elderly Sabzivārīs who still remembered the water system as it was about forty years ago, and the Sabzivār Master Plan.

9. During the 1950s, water pipes were laid out throughout Sabzivār and *jūb*s began to disappear. However, one can still see occasional cases of *kūchih*s with *jūb*s along their center lines. *Jūb*s now tend to drain the excess water during the rainy seasons.

10. For a good study of traditional Iranian houses, see Bonine (1980).

11. In some areas of Iran, such as the province of Khurāsān, the *sih-darī,* a room with three doors, is more popular..

12. For a scientific study of the *bād-gīr,* see Bahadori (1978).

3. Trade, Historical Events, and the City

1. Today in the Iranian province of Khurāsān (through which an important part of the old Silk Route passed) one can find some remains of Sassanian roads. A significant portion of the government income during the Sassanian Empire was obtained by levying taxes on the goods carried by caravans; thus, the rulers of this empire paid a great deal of attention to the improvement of trade roads by building *kārvānsarāy*s, qanats, wells, and so forth. See Ghirshman (1954).

2. For very early accounts of the Royal Road, see Komroff (1928: 282–283). See also Starr (1983; a map on p. 278 marking the boundaries of the Persian Empire illustrates the course of the Royal Road within the empire).

3. A good study of Iranian *kārvānsarāy*s can be found in Siroux (1949).

4. For an architectural study of the bazar of Iṣfahān, see Browne and Cantacuzino (1976).

5. "Colleges" here means *madrasih*s or religious schools.

6. For a good study of the bazar of Kirmān, see Frieden and Mann (1971).

7. This description of the bazar of Sabzivār is based on my own observations, interviews with local architects, elder citizens, and information from the Master Plan of Sabzivār prepared by the Ministry of Housing and Urban Planning in 1979–1980.

8. An early history of Sabzivār written during the twelfth century A.D. can be found in Baihaqi (1938). Baihaq (or Beihaq) was the old name for the city of Sabzivār.

9. Several larger Iranian cities like Tehran, Tabrīz, Iṣfahān, and Shīrāz

have traditionally contained a significant number of minorities such as Armenians, Assyrian Christians, Jews, Bahā'īs, and Zoroastrians.

10. However, in some cases, the constant competition to attract customers might lead to a bad relationship between two neighboring shopkeepers.

11. See Bonine (1981) and Keddie (1981b).

4. Religion, Sociopolitical Structures, and the City

1. For a brief survey of early religions in Iran, see Jackson (1906) and Frye (1963).

2. These three acts of purification are also present in the Aryan Hindu religion and its daughter religion, Buddhism. For a detailed study of Zoroastrianism, see Jackson (1898); Zaehner (1961), and Boyce (1977).

3. Even today, a careful visitor to Sāvih's mosque can observe the reddish color of the *miḥrāb*'s wall mixed with soot spots. This, plus the square pattern of the *miḥrāb*'s floor (pre-Islamic Iranian architectural style), clearly indicates that the whole structure was once the holy section of a former *ātashkadih,* where the sacred fire was kept burning. (Due to respect for the sacred fire, the walls of the holy section were painted red—the color of the fire.)

4. The Friday Mosque is not always the most important mosque of the city. In some cities that have served as major capitals, such as Iṣfahān and Tehran, there are other magnificent mosques built by kings or other royal families, and their importance often surpasses that of the Friday Mosque.

5. See Pope (1967: 3/906–911) for a discussion of the mosque. See also Von Grunebaum (1955).

6. A visitor to the mosque of Sāvih in the eleventh century referred to a great collection of astrolabes and globes for the study of astronomy, as well as a collection of books on different secular subjects housed in the mosque (Gibb and Kramers 1953).

7. The most recent example of a mosque built by a royal family is the beautiful mosque of the mother of the former shah, Muḥammad-Riżā Pahlavī, built in the city of Rey, south of Tehran.

8. This Zoroastrian belief was also adopted by some pre-Christian Jewish sects and by Christianity itself.

9. For a good study of Shiʿite Islam and its practice in Iran, see Sykes (1910). For a recent and comprehensive study of Shiʿites in Iran and Ḥusayn's tragedy, see Momen (1985). For a brief account of Imām Ḥusayn, see Faizi (1977).

10. The most comprehensive historical study of Mashhad is *Maṭlaʿ al-Shams,* written by Ṣaniʿ al-Daula (Davlih) in 1885 and reprinted in Tehran in 1983. See also Fraser (1825) and Sykes (1910).

11. Another Iranian city that could fit this model is Qum, also religiously based. Qum developed around the shrine of Maʿṣūmih, the sister of Imām Riżā, who in the ninth century was buried where the second holiest shrine in Iran now stands (the holiest being the shrine of Imām Riżā in Mashhad).

12. An example of this is the shrine of Ḥāj Mullā Hādī (Asrār) Sabzivārī in

the city of Sabzivār. He was an Islamic philosopher and poet who lived during the nineteenth century. His shrine today is one of the gathering places located at the eastern part of the city in the vicinity of the old city gate.

13. In larger Iranian cities the main *ḥusaynīyyih*s, as open squares along the bazar, are known as *takyih*s (*takya*s).

14. The high Zoroastrian priests (*muʾbadān* and *mughān*) were the closest advisers of the pre-Islamic Persian kings. During the Islamic period, the unity of state and church continued to be the same; religious leaders referred to kings as "the shadow of God on the Earth" (in reference to the famous hadith or Prophet Muḥammad's saying *al-Sulṭanuw Ẓill Allāh*, meaning kings are shadows of God).

15. Often the military leaders were the large landowners too; as we saw earlier, religious leaders were responsible for religious as well as secular education of the youth. For more information about the social and political structure of Iranian society, see Arasteh (1964) and Vreeland et al. (1957).

16. In the past, during the New Year celebration, different games (particularly royal polo), fireworks, plays, wrestling, and other activities took place in *maydān*s (Wilber 1975).

17. *Qahvih-khānih* literally means coffeehouse; however, in Iranian cities they mainly serve tea.

18. For a good understanding of the *zūr-khānih* and its related rituals, see Arasteh (1961).

19. When there was only one *ḥammām* in a neighborhood, it was used by men and women, but during different hours. For example, in Sabzivār, until about twenty years ago, the Ḥammām-i Ḥakīm was used from sunset to sunrise by men and during the day by women. *Ḥammām*s were one of the few public services that were privately owned. Their owners charged their customers for the usage of the *ḥammām*.

20. The *maḥallih* system no longer exists in its traditional sense in present Iranian cities, having given way to segregation by social and financial conditions. The rich now live in segregated suburbs, away from the poor. For example, in Tehran the houses in elevated areas with fresh air and cooler temperatures (such as those of Shamīrān) are occupied by wealthy populations in their own exclusive suburb, the *maḥallih* in a modern sense.

Appendix A

1. For further information on qanats, particularly their relationship to the physical geography of the Iranian Plateau, see the discussion of water and settlements in chapter 2.

2. A detailed study of traditional measurements and construction of qanats in Iran is found in Smith (1953).

Appendix B

1. Information for this section is based mainly on field observations and on the master plans for Iranian cities, available at the Ministry of Housing and Urban Development in Tehran.

2. For a historical study of *kārvānsarāys* and their architectural plans, see Pope (1967: 3/1245–1251).

Appendix C

1. For a good study of Iranian mosque architecture, see Pope (1967: 3/906–965).

2. It is possible that the concept of *miḥrāb* in Muslim mosques was borrowed either from the altar in Christian churches or from Jewish synagogues that faced Jerusalem.

3. For more information related to the Shah's Mosque in Iṣfahān, see Browne and Cantacuzino (1976) and Ardalan and Bakhtiar (1979).

4. Cases such as the Shah's Mosque are also seen in other Middle Eastern cities. Tourists in Istanbul, for example, cannot help being struck by the seemingly strange angles of many of the mosques in the old center of the city (these mosques were established in a Christian city where street patterns were already well established).

In some Islamic cities, according to several scholars, the orientation of the Friday Mosque determined the orientation of streets around them. Michael Bonine, in a paper presented at 1986 AAG Meetings (City Planning in Early Islamic Cities of the Maghrib), stated that the orientation of mosques determined the orientation of streets and the actual layout of several cities in the Maghrib.

GLOSSARY

***āb*:** water.
***āb-anbār*:** water cistern.
***āftāb*:** sunshine; sun.
***āftāb-gīr*:** sun catcher; room facing south in order to catch the maximum solar radiation during the cold winter days (also called *āftāb-rū*, literally meaning facing the sun).
Ahura Mazda (Ahūrāmazdā): the God of Light in Zoroastrianism—the popular pre-Islamic religion of Iranians—who according to followers is in a constant battle against the Ahriman, the God of Darkness.
ʿAlī: the Prophet Muḥammad's cousin and son-in-law and the fourth Righteous Caliph in Sunni Islam. According to Shiʿite Islam, ʿAlī was the true leader of the Muslim community after the Prophet Muḥammad's death, and he is the first of all Shiʿite *Imām*s.
ʿĀlī Qāpū: the palace of Shah ʿAbbas (seventeenth century) located in modern Iṣfahān by the Maydān-i Shāh.
Āqā: title of respect for any male meaning sir; more specifically used as a title for religious leaders.
***arg*:** the ruler's residence; usually the seat of the government in traditional Iranian cities (also citadel).
***ātashkadih*:** the Zoroastrian fire temple where the holy fire (Ātash-i Muqaddas) was supposed to be kept burning eternally.
***ayvān* (*iwan*):** a hallway usually facing north away from the sun in traditional Iranian houses; sometimes referred to as *tālār*.
***bād-gīr*:** wind catcher; chimneylike structure built in the roof of houses in arid regions to catch the pleasant winds and channel them down to cool the rooms.
***bād-i ṣad-uw-bīst rūzih*:** the destructive wind that blows over southeastern sections of Iran, lasting 120 (*ṣad-uw-bīst*) days.

bāgh: garden, park.

bāghchih: little garden, usually next to the pool in a traditional Iranian courtyard house.

Banī Hāshim: the clan to which the Prophet Muḥammad and the Twelve Shiʿite *Imāms* belonged.

bazar: a complex of linear (and usually covered) lanes; bounded by shops, *kārvānsarāys*, and main public centers, it forms the focus of the traditional Iranian city.

bāzārchih: small community bazar or small stretch of bazar, which is usually covered.

bāzār-i buzurg: the great bazar wider and longer than the others, usually giving access to smaller bazars and pathways.

bāzārī(s): the merchants, workers, and shopkeepers of the bazar.

bunbast: a blind alley usually giving access to several residential units.

chahār sū or ***chahār sūq***: a covered round or hexagonal space provided by the intersection of four different *rāstih-bāzārs*.

chāh-i āb: water well.

dallāk: the worker in a *ḥammām* who rubbed the dirt off the customer's body and often also worked as a masseur and barber.

dārūghih (***dārūgha***): the chief of police in traditional Iranian cities.

darvāzih (***darvāza***): usually the gate to the traditional walled city.

dasht: a plain (or any open field).

dastih: group; specifically the name for religious processions that move within the city in an orderly and formal fashion during the holy month of Muḥarram commemorating the martyrdom of Imām Husayn, the Third Shiʿite *Imām*. *Dastih* is also called *hayʾat*.

guzar: a major pathway, usually connecting a neighborhood center to the main city bazar.

ḥammām: bathhouse; in a traditional city, the public bathhouse.

hashtī: literally, octagonal, a covered space comprised of an entrance door to several residential units and an opening onto a pathway.

hayʾat: literally a group or *dastih*; more specifically, a union of people with a common interest.

hayʾat-i aṣnāf: union of guilds.

Ḥusayn (Hussein): the Third Shiʿite *Imām*; the second son of ʿAlī, and the grandson of Muḥammad, who—according to Shiʿite belief—was martyred (680 A.D.) in an uprising against the corrupted government of Yazīd, the second caliph of the Umayyad Empire.

ḥusaynīyyih (***ḥusaynīyya***): a building used during the month of Muḥarram to mourn and commemorate the martyrdom of Ḥusayn and his followers in the plain of Karbalā in Iraq.

imām (***emam***): (capitalized) the title for the twelve Shiʿite Muslim religious leaders in succession after Muḥammad the Prophet; (lowercase) a leader of congregational prayer or a learned man in Islamic science in Arabic.

imāmzādih (***imāmzāda***): the descendant of any of the Twelve Shiʿite *Imām*s; also the shrine in which an *Imām*'s descendant is buried.

jūb: an open water ditch running alongside or in the center line of traditional Iranian streets and alleys.
***kaʿba* (*kaʿbih*)**: the cubic house of God in Mecca, Saudi Arabia.
***kārvānī*(*s*)**: merchants, passengers, and workers of traditional caravans.
***kārvānsarāy* (*caravanserai*)**: house of the caravan; a building along the trade routes or within cities to provide lodging and commercial exchange facilities for members of caravans.
kavīr: barren salt deserts; specifically, the title for two deserts in the central Iranian Plateau.
khānih: house.
kishvar: country.
kūchih: literally, alley; in the traditional city it referred to any kind of pathway.
kūh: mountain.
***madrasih* (*madrasa*)**: school; usually defined as a religious school because there was no clear distinction between secular and religious studies in traditional Iranian schools.
***maḥallih* (*maḥalla*)**: a segregated neighborhood within a traditional city.
majmūʿih-yi bāzār: the bazar complex containing several bazars and their related public buildings.
masjid: mosque.
Masjid-i Jāmiʿ: the Congregational Mosque (see also Masjid-i Jumʿih).
Masjid-i Jumʿih: the Friday Mosque.
maydān: a large open public square, usually located at the center of Iranian cities.
mazār: a shrine of a saint.
***minārih* (*mināra*)**: minaret, usually the symbol of the mosque. The tall minaret helped visitors to the city to find their way to the mosque; it was also used for calling the faithful to prayer.
minbar: the pulpit where the religious leader sits when preaching.
muhr: a clay tablet made from the earth of sacred Shiʿite cities; used to mark the place on the floor for the forehead during prostration in prayer.
mullā: religious preacher and teacher.
Naqsh-i Jahān: the Image of the World; a large public square (*maydān*) built by Shah ʿAbbās I (seventeenth century) at the center of Iṣfahān (also called Maydān-i Shāh: the Royal Square).
***nisār* (*nesar*)**: the shady side of an Iranian house, usually facing north.
panj-darī: a common type of room with five doors.
pishnamāz: the leader of communal prayers, also called *imām*.
qanat: a subterranean aqueduct bringing fresh water by gravitational force from the bases of the mountains to settlements.
***qiblih* (*qibla*)**: direction of the Muslim Holy House (*kaʿba*) in Mecca, Saudi Arabia.
Qurʾān (Koran): the holy book of Muslims.
rāstih: a pathway (*guzar*), usually running in a straight line.
rāstih-bāzār: a linear stretch of bazar.

rūd: river.

sarāy: small *kārvānsarāy* located along the bazar reserved for commercial purposes.

Sayyid: a descendant of the Prophet (also referred to as Āqā).

shabistān: sanctuary hall of the mosque.

shahr: city.

Shiʿite (Shiʿa): a sect of Islam believing in the spiritual leadership of ʿAlī and his descendants after Muḥammad.

sih-darī: a common type of room with three doors.

tālār: a column-structured porch in Iranian houses, usually facing north in arid regions; also called *ayvān.*

ʿulamā: learned religious men (singular: *ʿālim*).

ustād: a skilled and experienced leader of apprentices (also a learned man, professor, etc.).

vaqf: religious endowment for charitable purposes (plural, *auqāf*).

zīr-zamīn: also called *sardāb,* basement of an Iranian house.

zūr-khānih: house of strength; the traditional Iranian sports club for training soul and body.

BIBLIOGRAPHY

Abu-Lughod, Janet. 1969. "Varieties of Urban Experience: Contrast, Coexistence, and Coalescence in Cairo." In Lapidus 1969.

———. 1987. "The Islamic City—Historic Myth, Islamic Essence, and Contemporary Relevance." *International Journal of Middle East Studies* 19: 155–176.

Ackerman, P., and A. U. Pope. 1967. "Gardens." In Pope 1967 (vol. 3).

Afshar, Iraj. 1969–1970. *Yadigār-hā-yi Yazd* [Monuments of Yazd]. Vol. 1. Tehran: n.p. (in Persian).

Alberts, Robert C. 1963. "Social Structure and Culture Change in an Iranian Village." Ph.D. dissertation, University of Wisconsin.

Algar, Hamid. 1969. *Religion and State in Iran, 1785–1906: The Role of Ulama in the Qajar Period.* Berkeley: University of California Press.

Al-Hathoul, Saleh. 1980. "Urban Forms in Arab-Muslim Cities." *Ekistics* 280: 15–16.

Al-Muqaddasi. 1906. *Ahsan al-tagāsīm fī Maʿrafat al-agālīm.* [The Best Division for the Classification of Regions]. Leiden: E. J. Brill (in Arabic).

Anderson, Stanford. 1980. "Conventions of Form and Conventions of Use in Urban Social Space." *Ekistics* 280: 31–35.

Anjana, P. Desai, V. Shah Sonal, and K. Shah Shymali. 1982. "Pre-Industrial Elements in the Industrial City of Ahmedabad." *Ekistics* 295: 320–323.

Arasteh, A. Reza. 1961. "The Social Role of the *Zūr-khānih* (House of Strength) in Iranian Urban Communities during the Nineteenth Century." *Der Islam* 37: 256–259.

———. 1964. *Man and Society in Iran.* Leiden: E. J. Brill.

Arberry, Arthur J. 1960. *Shiraz: Persian City of Saints and Poets.* Centers of Civilization Series, vol. 2. Norman: University of Oklahoma Press.

Ardalan, Nader, and Laleh Bakhtiar. 1979. *The Sense of Unity: The Sufi Tra-*

dition in Persian Architecture. Publications of the Center for Middle Eastern Studies, no. 9. Chicago: University of Chicago Press.

Ashraf, Ahmad. 1974. "Vīzhigī-hā-yi Tārīkhī-yi Shahrnishīnī dar Īran-i Dauri-yi Islāmī" [The Historical Characteristics of Urbanization in the Islamic Period of Iran]. *Nāmih-yi ʿUlūm-i Ijtimāʿī* 4: 7–47 (in Persian).

Atlas of Iran. 1971. Tehran: Saḥāb Geographic and Drafting Institute.

Atlas of the Middle East. 1975. Dubuque, Ia.: Kendall/Hunt Publishing.

Baali, Faud, and Ali Wardi. 1981. *Ibn Khaldun and Islamic Thought-Styles: A Social Perspective.* Boston: G. K. Hall.

Badiʿi, Rabiʿ. 1983. *Jughrāfiyā-yi Mufaṣṣal-i Īrān* [A Detailed Geography of Iran]. 3 vols. Tehran: Eqbāl Publications (in Persian).

Bahadori, M. N. 1978. "Passive Cooling Systems in Iranian Architecture." *Scientific American* 238: 144–154.

Bahar, Mehrdad. 1976. "Varzish-i Bāstānī-yi Īrān va Rīshih-hā-yi Tārīkhī-yi ān" [Ancient Sports and Their Historical Roots in Iran]. *Zūr-khānih-hā-yi Tihran* [Traditional Sports Clubs of Tehran] 42: 5–30 (in Persian).

Baihaqi, A. A. Z. 1938. *Tārīkh-i Baihaq* [History of Baihaq (Old Sabzivār)]. Tehran: Canūn Press (in Persian).

Bakhtiar, Ali. 1974. *Studies on Isfahan.* Edited by Renata Holod. Boston: Society for Iranian Studies.

Balkhi, A. A. 1971. *Fażāyil-i Balkh* [Virtues of the Balkh]. Tehran: Bunyād-i Farhang-i Īrān (in Persian).

Bartold, W. 1984. *A Historical Geography of Iran.* Translated by Suat Soucek. Princeton: Princeton University Press.

Bastani Parizi, M. E. 1979. *Ḥimāsih-yi Kavīr* [The Epic of Kavīr]. Tehran: Amīr-kabīr Publication (in Persian).

Bavar, Syrus. 1983. "Urban Form as Physical Expression of Social Structure in Arid Zones of Iran." In Golany 1983.

Bazin, Marcel. 1973. "Qom, ville de pèlerinage et centre régional." *Revue Géographique de l'Est* 13:1/2: 77–136.

Beaudouin, E. E., and A. U. Pope. 1967. "City Plans." In Pope 1967 (3/1391–1410).

Beaumont, Peter. 1968. "Qanats on the Varamin Plain, Iran." *Institute of British Geographers* 45: 169–179.

———. 1971. "Qanat System in Iran." *Bulletin of the International Association of Scientific Hydrology* 16: 39–50.

———. 1974. "Water Resource Development in Iran." *Geographical Journal* 140: 418–431.

Beaumont, Peter, G. H. Blake, and J. M. Wagstaff. 1978. *The Middle East: A Geographical Study.* New York: John Wiley and Sons.

Beazley, E. 1977. "Some Vernacular Buildings of the Iranian Plateau." *Iran* 15: 89–102.

Beazley, E., and M. Haverson. 1982. *Living with the Desert: Working Buildings of the Iranian Plateau.* Warminster Wilts, England: Aris and Phillips, Teddington House.

Beckett, Philip H. T. 1951. "Waters of Persia." *Geographical Magazine* 24: 230–240.

———. 1966. "The City of Kerman, Iran." *Erdkunde* 20/2: 119–125.

Beckett, P. H. T., and E. D. Gordon. 1966. "Land Use and Settlement round Kerman in Southern Iran." *Geographical Journal* 132/4: 476–490.

Behnam, Jamshid. 1968. "Population." In *Cambridge History of Iran*. Vol. 1. Cambridge: Cambridge University Press.

Bemont, Fredy. 1969. *Les villes de l'Iran, dès cités d'autrefois à l'urbanisme contemporain*. 2 vols. Paris: by the author; reprint ed. 1973.

Benet, F. 1954. "The Ideology of Islamic Urbanization." *Economic Development and Cultural Change* 3: 211–226.

Bill, James Alban. 1972. *The Politics of Iran: Groups, Classes and Modernization*. Columbus, Ohio: Charles E. Merrill.

Blake, G. H., and R. I. Lawless. 1980. *The Changing Middle Eastern City*. New York: Barnes and Noble Books.

Bobek, H. 1958. "Tehran." *Geographische Forschungen* 190: 5–24.

Bonine, Michael E. 1975. *Yazd and Its Hinterland: A Central Place System of Dominance in the Central Iranian Plateau*. Austin: University of Texas at Austin, Department of Geography.

———. 1977. "From Uruk to Casablanca: Perspectives on the Urban Experience of the Middle East." *Journal of Urban History* 3: 141–180.

———. 1979. "The Morphogenesis of Iranian Cities." *Annals of the Association of American Geographers* 69: 208–224.

———. 1980. "Aridity and Structure: Adaptations of Indigenous Housing in Iran." In Clark and Paylore 1980.

———. 1981. "Shops and Shopkeepers: Dynamics of an Iranian Provincial Bazaar." In *Modern Iran: The Dialectics of Continuity and Change*. Edited by Michael Bonine and Nikki Keddie. Albany: State University of New York Press.

———. 1983. "Cities of the Middle East and North Africa." In *Cities of the World*. Edited by Stanley D. Brunn and Jack Williams. New York: Harper and Row.

Bosworth, Edmund. 1971. *Iran and Islam*. Edinburgh: Edinburgh University Press.

Bosworth, Edmund, and Carole Hillenbrand. 1983. *Qajar Iran: Political, Social and Cultural Change 1800–1925*. Edinburgh: Edinburgh University Press.

Boyce, Mary. 1977. *A Persian Stronghold of Zoroastrianism*. Oxford: Clarendon Press.

Boyle, J. A. 1968. *The Saljuq and Mongol Periods*. Vol. 5 of the *Cambridge History of Iran*. Cambridge: Cambridge University Press.

Broadbent, Geoffrey. 1980. "Meaning in the Islamic Environment." *Ekistics* 280: 78.

Brown, Carl. 1973. *From Madina to Metropolis: Heritage and Change in the Near Eastern City*. Princeton: Darwin Press.

Brown, Judith A. 1968. "Kerman: A Desert Town in Iran." In *Asian Sample Studies*. Sheffield: Geographical Association.

Browne, E. G. 1910. *The Persian Revolution 1905–1909*. Cambridge: Cambridge University Press.

Browne, Kenneth, and Sherban Cantacuzino. 1976. "Isfahan." *Architectural Review* 159 (Iran issue).
Butler, Millard. 1933. "Irrigation in Persia by Kanats." *Civil Engineering* 3: 69–73.
Clark, Brian A., and Vincent Costello. 1973. "The Urban System and Social Patterns in Iranian Cities." *Transactions of the Institute of British Geographers* 58: 99–128.
Clark, Kenneth N., and Patricia Paylore. 1980. *Desert Housing: Balancing Experience and Technology for Dwelling in Hot Arid Zones.* Tucson: University of Arizona, Office of Arid Lane Studies.
Clarke, John I. 1966. *The Iranian City of Shiraz.* Department of Geography Research Paper Series, no. 7. Durham: University of Durham.
Clarke, John, and Brian Clark. 1969. *Kermanshah: An Iranian Provincial City.* Department of Geography Research Paper Series, no. 10. Durham: University of Durham.
Connell, John (ed.). 1969. *Semnan: Persian City and Region.* London: University College.
Coon, Carleton S. 1958. *Caravans: The Story of the Middle East.* New York: Henry Holt.
Costa, Frank J., and Ahmed Moustapha. 1983. "Suggested Elements of a Building Code for Islamic Communities." *Ekistics* 298: 24–29.
Costello, V. F. 1976. *Kashan: A City and Region of Iran.* Epping, Essex: Bowker.
Cressey, George. 1958. "Qanats, Karez, and Faggaras." *Geographical Review* 47: 27–44.
Curzon, George N. 1966. *Persia and the Persian Question.* 2 vols. London: Frank Cass.
Danby, Miles. 1980. "The Islamic Architectural Tradition and the House." *Ekistics* 280: 46–50.
Elkabir, Yassin Ali. 1983. "The Study of Urbanization in the Arab World: A Theoretical Perspective." *Ekistics* 300: 232–236.
Encyclopaedia of Islam. New ed. Leiden: E. J. Brill, 1975.
English, Paul Ward. 1966a. *City and Village in Iran: Settlement and Economy in the Kirman Basin.* Madison: University of Wisconsin Press.
———. 1966b. "Culture Change and the Structure of a Persian City." *Texas Quarterly* 9: 158–171.
———. 1968. "The Origin and Spread of Qanats in the Old World." *American Philosophical Society* 112: 170–181.
———. 1973. "The Traditional City of Herat, Afghanistan." In Brown 1973.
Faizi, Abu'l-Qasim. 1977. *The Prince of Martyrs: A Brief Account of the Imam Husayn.* Oxford: George Ronald.
Falamaki, Mansour. 1977. *Bāz-zindih Sāzī-yi Bānā-hā va Shahr-hā-yi Tārīkhī* [Restoration of the Ancient Buildings and Cities]. Tehran: University of Tehran Press (in Persian).
———. 1978. *Siyrī dar Tajārub-i Marammat-i Shahrī: Az Vinīz tā Shīrāz* [An Essay on Urban Conservation: From Venice to Shīrāz] Tehran: Ābān Publications (in Persian).

Fathi, Hassan. 1973. "Constancy, Transposition and Change in the Arab City." In Brown 1973.

———. 1986. *Natural Energy and Vernacular Architecture: Principles and Examples with Preference to Hot Arid Climates.* Chicago: University of Chicago Press.

Fischer, Michael M. J. 1973. "Zoroastrian Iran: Between Myth and Praxis." Ph.D. dissertation, University of Chicago.

———. 1980. *Iran: From Religious Dispute to Revolution.* Cambridge: Harvard University Press.

Fisher, William B. (ed.). 1968. "Physical Geography." In *Cambridge History of Iran.* Vol. 1: *The Land of Iran.* Cambridge: Cambridge University Press.

Floor, W. M. 1971. "The Office of the Kalantar in Qajar, Persia." *Journal of the Economic and Social History of the Orient* 14: 253–269.

Fraser, James B. 1825. *Narrative of a Journey into Khorasan, in the Years 1821 and 1822.* London: Longman, Hurst, Rees, Orme, Brown, and Green.

Frieden, Ray A., and Bruce D. Mann. 1971. *Strategy for Sound Adaptation and Development: A Case Study of Kerman Bazaar.* Tehran: Ministry of Interior.

———. 1974. "New Influences on Persian Cities: A Case Study of Kerman, Iran." *Architects' Yearbook* 14: 46–53.

Frye, Richard N. 1963. *The Heritage of Persia.* New York: World Publishing.

Ganji, Mohammad Hassan. 1968. "Climate." In *Cambridge History of Iran.* Vol. 1: *The Land of Iran.* Cambridge: Cambridge University Press.

Gaube, Heinz. 1979. *Iranian Cities.* New York: New York University Press.

Ghirshman, R. 1954. *Iran: From the Earliest Times to the Islamic Conquest.* Baltimore: Penguin Books.

Gibb, H. A. R., and J. H. Kramers. 1953. *Shorter Encyclopaedia of Islam.* New York: Cornell University Press.

Goblot, H. 1979. *Les qanats: Une technique d'acquisition de l'eau.* Paris: Mouton.

Golany, Gideon S. 1978. *Urban Planning for Arid Zones (American Experiences and Directions).* New York: John Wiley and Sons.

———. 1980. *Housing in Arid Lands.* London: Architectural Press.

———. 1981. "Arid Zone Settlement Site Selection: The Case of Egypt." *Ekistics* 291: 456–466.

———. 1982. *Desert Planning.* London: Architectural Press.

———. 1983. *Design for Arid Regions.* New York: Van Nostrand Reinhold.

Grabar, Oleg. 1969. "The Architecture of the Middle Eastern City." In Lapidus 1969.

Greenshields, T. H. 1980. "Quarter and Ethnicity." In Lawless and Blake 1980.

Hakim, B. S. 1986. *Arabic-Islamic Cities: Buildings and Planning Principles.* New York: Routledge and Kegan Paul.

Hamdan, G. 1962. "The Pattern of Medieval Urbanism in the Arab World." *Geography* 47: 121–134.

Harrison, J. V. 1968. "Geology." In *Cambridge History of Iran.* Vol. 1: *The Land of Iran.* Cambridge: Cambridge University Press.

Hassan, Riaz. 1971. "The Nature of Islamic Urbanization: A Historical Perspective." *Ekistics* 182: 61–63.

———. 1972. "Islam and Urbanization in the Medieval Middle East." *Ekistics* 195: 108–112.

Herodotus. 1958. *The Histories of Herodotus of Halicanassus.* Translated by Harry Carter. New York: Heritage Press.

Herzfield, Ernest E. 1935. *Archaeological History of Iran.* London: Oxford University Press.

Hillenbrand, Robert. 1971. "Mosques and Mausolea in Khurasan and Central Iran." *Iran: Journal of the British Institute of Persian Studies* 9: 160–162.

Hitchcock, Veronica. 1974. "The City of the Sacred Flame, Yazd, Iran." *Country Life* (31 October): 1263–1267.

Holt, P. M., Ann K. S. Lambton, and Bernard Lewis. 1970. *The Cambridge History of Islam.* 2 vols. Cambridge: Cambridge University Press.

Hourani, A. H., and S. M. Stern. 1970. *The Islamic City: A Colloquium.* Oxford: Bruno Cassirer.

Hunarfar, Lutfullah. 1978. *Iṣfahān.* Tehran: Sipihr Publications (in Persian).

Ibn Batuta. 1958. *Safarnāmih* [Travel Account]. Translated by M. A. Muvahhid. Tehran: Bungāh-i Tarjumih va Nashr-i Kitāb (in Persian).

Ibn Khaldun. 1980. *The Muqaddamah: An Introduction to History.* 3 vols. Translated by Franz Rosenthal. New York: Bollingen Foundation.

Ismail, Adel A. 1972. "Origin, Ideology and Physical Patterns of Arab Urbanization." *Ekistics* 195: 113–121.

Issavi, Charles. 1971. *The Economic History of Iran: 1800–1914.* Chicago: University of Chicago Press.

Istakhri, Abu Ishaq. 1870. *Masalik val Mamalik* [The Affairs of Countries]. Edited by Michael Jan de Goeje. Leiden: E. J. Brill (in Arabic).

Jackson, A. V. W. 1898. *Zoroaster, the Prophet of Ancient Iran.* New York: Columbia University Press.

———. 1906. *Persia Past and Present: A Book of Travel and Research.* New York: Macmillan.

———. 1911. *From Constantinople to the Home of Omar Khayyam.* New York: Macmillan.

Javadi, A. (ed.). 1984. *Miʿmārī-yi Īrān* [Iranian Architecture]. 2 vols. Tehran: Mujarrad Publications (in Persian).

Kamiar, Mohammad. 1983. "The Qanat System in Iran." *Ekistics* 303: 467–472.

Keddie, Nikki. 1981a. "Religion, Society, and Revolution in Modern Iran." In *Modern Iran: The Dialectics of Continuity and Change.* Edited by Michael E. Bonine and Nikki Keddie. Albany: State University of New York.

———. 1981b. *Roots of Revolution: An Interpretive History of Modern Iran.* New Haven: Yale University Press.

Kiani, M. Y. (ed.). 1986. *Nazarī Ijmālī bih Shahr-nishīnī va Shahr-sāzī dar Īrān* [A General Study on Urbanization and Urban Planning in Iran]. Tehran: Irshād-i Islāmī (in Persian).

———. 1987. *Shahr-hā-yi Īrān* [Iranian Cities]. Tehran: Sāzimān-i Chāp va Intishārāt-i Vizārat-i Farhang va Irshād-i Islāmī [Ministry of Islamic Guidance Press] (in Persian).

Kinneir, J. M. 1973. *Geographical Memoir of the Persian Empire.* New York: Arno Press.

Kish, George. 1978. *A Source Book in Geography.* Cambridge: Harvard University Press.

Komroff, Manuel (ed.). 1928. *The History of Herodotus.* New York: Tudor Publishing.

Lamberg-Karlovsky, C. C., and Martha Lamberg-Karlovsky. 1971. "An Early City in Iran." *Scientific American* 224: 102–112.

Lambton, Ann K. S. 1953. *Landlord and Peasant in Persia: A Study of Land Tenure and Revenue Administration.* Oxford: Oxford University Press.

———. 1969. *Persian Vocabulary.* Cambridge: Cambridge University Press.

Lampl, Paul. 1968. *Cities and Planning in the Ancient Near East.* New York: George Braziller.

Lapidus, I. M. 1967. *Muslim Cities in the Later Middle Ages.* Cambridge: Harvard University Press.

———. 1969. *Middle Eastern Cities: A Symposium on Ancient, Islamic, and Contemporary Middle Eastern Urbanism.* Berkeley: University of California Press.

———. 1973. "The Evolution of Muslim Urban Society." *Comparative Studies in Society and History* 15: 21–50.

Lawless, G. H., and G. H. Blake (eds.). 1980. *The Changing Middle Eastern City.* New York: Harper and Row.

Lebon, J. H. G. 1971. "The Islamic City in the Near East." *Ekistics* 182: 64–71.

Le Strange, Guy. 1977. *The Lands of the Eastern Caliphate.* Lahore: Al-biruni.

Lewis, Peter G. 1983. "Iranian Cities." *Focus* 33: 12–16.

Lockhart, Laurence. 1939. *Famous Cities of Iran.* Brentford: W. Pearce.

———. 1960. *Persian Cities.* London: Luzac.

Loeb, Laurence D. 1981. "The Religious Dimension of Modernization among the Jews of Shiraz." In *Modern Iran: The Dialectics of Continuity and Change.* Edited by Michael Bonine and Nikki Keddie. Albany: State University of New York.

Maheu, Rene. 1976. *Iran: Rebirth of a Timeless Empire.* Paris: Editions J. A.

Malcolm, John. 1815. *The History of Persia.* 2 vols. London: John Murray.

Marcais, Georges. 1945. "La conception des villes dans l'Islam." *Revue d'Alger* 2: 517–533.

Marcais, William. 1928. "L'Islamisme et la vie urbaine." *L'Académie des Inscriptions et Belles-Lettres, Comptes Rendus* (Paris, January–March): 86–100.

Matheson, Sylvia. 1972. *Persia: An Archaeological Guide.* London: Faber and Faber.

Mazzaoui, Michel. 1966. "Shiism and the Rise of Safavid." Ph.D. dissertation, Princeton University.

Ministry of Housing and Urban Development [Iran]. 1969. *Tarh-i Jāmiᶜ-i Mashhad* [Mashhad Master Plan]. Tehran: ACPU (in Persian).
———. 1972. *Ṭarḥ-i Jāmiᶜ-i Shīrāz* [Shīrāz Master Plan]. Tehran: ACPU (in Persian).
———. 1973. *Ṭarḥ-i Jāmiᶜ-i Irāk* [Irāk Master Plan]. Tehran: ACPU (in Persian).
———. 1974. *Ṭarḥ-i Jāmiᶜ-i Zanjān* [Zanjān Master Plan]. Tehran: ACPU (in Persian).
———. 1975a. *Ṭarḥ-i Jāmiᶜ-i Āmūl* [Āmūl Master Plan]. Tehran: ACPU (in Persian).
———. 1975b. *Ṭarḥ-i Jāmiᶜ-i Kirmān* [Kirmān Master Plan]. Tehran: ACPU (in Persian).
———. 1975c. *Ṭarḥ-i Jāmiᶜ-i Yazd* [Yazd Master Plan]. Tehran: ACPU (in Persian).
———. 1979. *Ṭarḥ-i Jāmiᶜ-i Sabzivār* [Sabzivār Master Plan]. Tehran: ACPU (in Persian).
———. 1981. *Ṭarḥ-i Jāmiᶜ-i Bujnūrd* [Bujnūrd Master Plan]. Tehran: ACPU (in Persian).
Ministry of Roads [Iran]. 1971. *Roads and Road Construction: From Achaemenian Era until the Reign of Pahlavis.* Tehran: Public Relations Department.
Momen, Moojan. 1985. *An Introduction to Shiᶜa Islam: The History and Doctrine of Twelver Shiᶜism.* Oxford: George Ronald.
Morris, J., R. Wood, and D. Wright. 1969. *Persia.* London: Thames and Hudson.
Mumford, Lewis. 1961. *The City in History.* New York: HBJ.
Najmi, Naser. 1983. *Īrān-i Qadīm va Tihrān-i Qadīm* [The Old Iran and the Old Tehran]. Tehran: Jānzādih Publications (in Persian).
Narshakhi. 1972. *Tārīkh-i Bukhārā* [History of Bukhārā]. Tehran: Bunyād-i Farhang-i Īrān (in Persian).
Naser, Khosrou. 1971. *Safarnāmih* [Travel Account]. Tehran: Kitāb-hā-yi Jībī (in Persian).
Nasr, Hoseyn S. 1964. *An Introduction to Islamic Cosmological Doctrines.* Cambridge: Harvard University Press.
———. 1966. *Ideas and Realities of Islam.* London: Allen and Unwin.
———. 1968a. *The Encounter of Man and Nature.* London: Allen and Unwin.
———. 1968b. "Man in the Universe: Permanence amid Apparent Change." *Studies in Comparative Religion* 2: 60–64.
———. 1976. *Islamic Science: An Illustrated Study.* n.p.: World of Islam Festival Publishing.
Noel, E. 1944. "Qanats." *Journal of the Central Asian Study* 31: 191–202.
Nyrope, R., W. Smith, et al. 1978. *Iran: A Country Study.* Washington, D.C.: American University.
Oberlander, T. M. 1965. *The Zagros Streams.* Syracuse Geographical Series. Syracuse: Syracuse University Press.
———. 1968. "Hydrography." In *Cambridge History of Iran.* Vol. 1: *The*

Land of Iran. Cambridge: Cambridge University Press.

Olgyay, Victor. 1963. *Design with Climate*. Princeton: Princeton University Press.

Pauty, E. 1951. "Villes spontanées et villes créées en Islam." *Annales de l'Institut d'Etudes Orientales* 9: 52–75.

Peusner, N., J. Fleming, and H. Honour. 1976. *A Dictionary of Architecture*. New York: Overlook Press.

Pigulevskaja, N. 1963. *Les villes de l'état Iranien*. Paris: Mouton.

Planhol, X. de. 1959. *The World of Islam*. Ithaca: Cornell University Press.

———. 1964a. "Abadan: Morphologie et fonction du tissu urbain." *Revue Géographique de l'Est* 4: 338–385.

———. 1964b. *Recherches sur la géographie humaine de l'Iran septentrional*. Paris: Centre de Recherches et Documentation Cartographiques.

———. 1968. "Geography of Settlement." In *Cambridge History of Iran*. Vol. 1: *The Land of Iran*. Cambridge: Cambridge University Press.

Pope, Arthur Upham. 1965. *Persian Architecture: The Triumph of Form and Color*. New York: George Braziller.

——— (ed.). 1967. *A Survey of Persian Art*. 6 vols. London: Oxford University Press (2nd impression).

Pour-Afkari, Nasrullah. 1980. "Shīvih-hā-yi Sunnatī-yi Taqsīm-i Āb dar Īrān" [The Traditional Ways of Water Distribution in Iran]. *Hunar va Mardum* [Art and People] 193: 48–51 (in Persian).

Qumi, H. M. 1934. *Tārīkh-i Qum* [History of Qum]. Tehran: Majlis Publications (in Persian).

Rabubi, Mustafa. 1980. "Sāmān-dahī-yi Bāzār" [Regularizing the Bazar]. *Asar* [Vestige] 2–4: 7–54 (in Persian).

Rabubi, Mustafa, and Frangis Rahimiyyih. 1974. *Shinākht-i Shahr va Maskan-i Būmī dar Īrān* [Understanding the City and Vernacular Dwelling in Iran]. Tehran: Zībā Publications (in Persian).

Rapopert, A. 1969. *House Form and Culture*. Englewood Cliffs, N.J.: Prentice-Hall.

Roberts, M. H. P. 1979. *An Urban Profile of the Middle East*. New York: St. Martin's Press.

Rotblat, Howard J. 1975. "Social Organization and Development in an Iranian Provincial Bazaar." *Economic Development and Cultural Change* 23: 292–305.

Royce, William. 1981. "The Shirazi Provincial Elite: Status Maintenance and Change." In *Modern Iran: The Dialectics of Continuity and Change*. Edited by Michael Bonine and Nikki Keddie. Albany: State University of New York Press.

Saʿidi, Abbas R. 1989. *Bīnish-i Islāmī va Padīdih-hā-yi Jughrāfiāyī: Muqaddamih-ī bar Jughrāfiyā-yi sarzamīn-hā-yi Islāmī* [Islamic Ideology and Geographical Phenomena: An Introduction to the Geography of Islamic Territories]. Mashhad: Āstān-i Quds-i Rażavī (Bunyād-i Pazhūhish-hā-yi Islāmī) [Islamic Research Foundation] (in Persian).

Saʿidiyan Abdul-Husayn. 1984. *Dāyirat al-Maʿārif-i Sarzamīn va Mardum-i*

Īrān [Encyclopaedia of Land and People of Iran]. Tehran: Elm va Zindigī Publications (in Persian).

Sami, Ali. 1977. "Shahr-i Bāstānī-yi Gūr va Fīrūzābād-i Kunūnī" [The Ancient City of Gur and the Present Fīrūzābād]. *Hunar va Mardum* 167: 2–9 (in Persian).

Ṣaniʿ al-Daula, Muḥammad Hasan Khan. 1885. *Matlaʿ al-Shams* [Where the Sun Rises]. Rpt. Tehran: Farhangsarā, 1983 (in Persian).

Saqqaf, Abdulaziz (ed.). 1987. *The Middle East City: Ancient Traditions Confront a Modern World.* New York: Paragon House.

Sauvaget, Jean. 1934. "Esquisse d'une histoire de la ville de Damas." *Revue des Etudes Islamiques* 8: 421–480.

———. 1941. *Alèp: Essai sur le développement d'une grande ville Syrienne, des origines au milieu de XIXe siècle.* 2 vols. Paris: P. Geuthner.

Savory, Roger. 1980. *Iran under the Safavids.* Cambridge: Cambridge University Press.

Scharlau, Kurt. 1961. "Moderne Umgestaltungen im Grundriss Iranischer Städte." *Erdkunde* 15: 180–191.

Schweizer, Gunther. 1972. "Tabriz (Nordwest-Iran) und der Tabrizer Bazar." *Erdkunde* 26: 32–46.

Serageldin, Ismail, and Samir El-Sadek (eds.). 1982. *The Arab City: Its Character and Islamic Cultural Heritage* (Proceedings of a Symposium held in Madina, Kingdom of Saudi Arabia, 28 February–5 March 1981 A.D.), Riyadh: Arab Urban Development Institute.

Shukuʾi, Hosayn. 1977. *Jughrāfiyā-yi Shahrī* [Urban Geography]. Tabrīz: University of Tabrīz Press (in Persian).

Siroux, Maxime. 1949. *Caravanserais d'Iran et petites constructions routières.* Cairo: Institut Français d'Archéologie Orientale.

Sjoberg, Gideon. 1960. *The Pre-Industrial City: Past and Present.* New York: Free Press.

Smith, Anthony. 1953. *Blind White Fish in Persia.* New York: Dutton.

Smith, C. G. 1970. "Water Resources and Irrigation Developments in the Middle East." *Geography* 55: 407–425.

Smith, E. B. 1950. *The Dome: A Study in the History of Ideas.* Princeton, N.J.: Princeton University Press.

Smith, Harvey. 1971. *The Area Handbook for Iran.* Washington, D.C.: American University.

Sopher, David E. 1967. *Geography of Religions.* Englewood Cliffs, N.J.: Prentice-Hall.

Spooner, B. J. 1963. "The Function of Religion in Persian Society." *Iran: Journal of the British Institute of Persian Studies* 1: 83–95.

———. 1971. "Religion and Society Today: An Anthropological Perspective." In *Iran Faces the Seventies.* Edited by Ehsan Yar-Shater. New York: Praeger Publishers.

Starr, C. G. 1983. *History of the Ancient World.* Oxford: Oxford University Press.

Stevens, Roger. 1979. *The Land of the Great Sophy.* New York: Taplinger Publishing.

Sultanzadih, Hosayn. 1983. *Ravand-i Shikl-Gīrī-yi Shahr va Marākiz-i Mazhabī dar Īrān* [Development of Cities and Religious Centers in Iran]. Tehran: Āgāh Publications (in Persian).

Sykes, Percy M. 1910. *The Glory of the Shiʿa World.* London: Macmillan.

———. 1930. *A History of Persia.* 2 vols. London: Macmillan.

Ṭabaṭaba'i, S. M. H. 1975. *Shiʿite Islam.* Albany: State University of New York Press.

Tahvildar, Mirza Hoseyn. 1966. *Jughrāfiyā-yi Iṣfahān* [Geography of Iṣfahān]. Tehran: Markaz-i Mutāliʿāt va Tahqīqāt-i Ijtimāʿī (MMTE) (in Persian).

Tavassoli, Mahmood. 1982. *Sākht-i Shahr va Miʿmārī dar Iqlīm-i Garm va Khushk-i Īrān* [Urban Structure and Architecture in the Hot Arid Zone Of Iran]. Tehran: University of Tehran Press (in Persian).

———. 1983. "City Planning in the Hot, Dry Climate of Iran." In Golany 1983.

Tekeli, Ilhan. 1971. "The Evolution of Spatial Organization in the Ottoman Empire and the Turkish Republic." *Ekistics* 182: 57–60.

Thompson, Tom C. 1981. "Petty Traders in Iran." In *Modern Iran: The Dialectics of Continuity and Change.* Edited by Michael Bonine and Nikki Keddie. Albany: State University of New York Press.

Varjavand, Parviz. 1977. "Istimrār-i Hunar-i Miʿmārī va Shahr-sāzī-yi Īrān-i Pīsh az Islām dar Daurān-i Islāmī" [Continuity of the Pre-Islamic Iranian Architecture in Islamic Periods]. *Hunar va Mardum* [Art and People] 180: 2–19 (in Persian).

———. 1978. "Naqsh va Ahamīyyat-i Birkih-hā va Āb-anbār-hā dar Bāft-i Shahr-hā-yi Īrānī" [The Role and Importance of the Water Channels and Water Cisterns in the Structure of Iranian Cities]. *Hunar va Mardum* [Art and People] 168: 2–6 (in Persian).

Verlag, C. W. L. 1966. *Die Entwicklang der Stadt Tehran.* Cologne: Klischees Peukert.

Von Grunebaum, G. E. 1955. *Islam: Essays in the Nature and Growth of a Cultural Tradition.* London: Routledge and Kegan Paul.

Vreeland, Herbert, et al. 1957. *Iran.* New Haven: Human Relations Area Files.

Wheatley, Paul. 1976. "Levels of Space Awareness in the Traditional Islamic City." *Ekistics* 42: 354–366.

Wickens, G. M. 1976. "Introduction to the Middle East." In *Introduction to Islamic Civilization.* Edited by R. M. Savory. Cambridge: Cambridge University Press.

Wilber, D. N. 1962. *Persian Gardens and Garden Pavilions.* Rutland, Vt.: C. E. Tuttle.

———. 1975. *Iran: Past and Present.* Princeton, N.J.: Princeton University Press.

Winters, Christopher. 1977. "Traditional Urbanism in the North Central Sudan." *Annals of the Association of American Geographers* 67: 500–520.

Wirth, Eugen. 1968. "Strukturwandlungen und Entwicklungstendenzen der Orientalischen Stadt." *Erdkunde* 22: 101–128.

Wulff, H. E. 1966. *The Traditional Crafts of Persia: Their Development, Technology and Influence on Eastern and Western Countries.* Cambridge: MIT Press.

———. 1968. "The Qanats of Iran." *Scientific American* 218: 94–105.

Zaehner, R. C. 1961. *The Dawn and Twilight of Zoroastrianism.* New York: G. P. Putnam's Sons.

INDEX